Three Plays of Euripides: Alcestis, Medea, The Bachae

by

Euripides

www.books.com.co

TABLE OF CONTENTS

Alcestis

Dramatis Personae

APOLLO
DEATH
CHORUS OF OLD MEN
A WOMAN SERVANT
ALCESTIS, the Queen, wife of ADMETUS
ADMETUS, King of Thessaly
EUMELUS, their child
HERACLES
PHERES, father of ADMETUS

At Pherae, outside the Palace of ADMETUS, King of
Thessaly. The centre of the scene represents a portico with
columns and a large double-door. To the left are the women's
quarters, to the right the guest rooms. The centre doors of
the Palace slowly open inwards, and Apollo comes out. In his
left hand he carries a large unstrung golden bow. He moves
slowly and majestically, turns, and raises his right hand in
salutation to the Palace.

APOLLO Dwelling of Admetus, wherein I, a God, deigned
to accept the food of serfs!

The cause was Zeus. He struck Asclepius, my son, full in
the breast with a bolt of thunder, and laid him dead. Then
in wild rage I slew the Cyclopes who forge the fire of Zeus.
To atone for this my Father forced me to labour as a hireling
for a mortal man; and I came to this country, and tended
oxen for my host. To this hour I have protected him and his.

I, who am just, chanced on the son of Pheres, a just man, whom I have saved from Death by tricking the Fates. The Goddesses pledged me their faith Admetus should escape immediate death if, in exchange, another corpse were given to the Under-Gods.

One by one he tested all his friends, and even his father and the old mother who bad brought him forth-and found none that would die for him and never more behold the light of day, save only his wife. Now, her spirit waiting to break loose, she droops upon his arm within the house; this is the day when she must die and render up her life.

But I must leave this Palace's dear roof, for fear pollution soil me in the house.

See! Death, Lord of All the Dead, now comes to lead her to the house of Hades! Most punctually he comes! How well he marked the day she had to die! (From the right comes DEATH, with a drawn sword in his hand. He moves stealthily towards the Palace; then sees APOLLO and halts abruptly. The two Deities confront each other.)

DEATH Ha! Phoebus! You! Before this Palace! Lawlessly would you grasp, abolish the rights of the Lower Gods! Did you not beguile the Fates and snatch Admetus from the grave? Does not that suffice? Now, once again, you have armed your hand with the bow, to guard the daughter of Pelias who must die in her husband's stead!

APOLLO Fear not! I hold for right, and proffer you just words.

DEATH If you hold for right, why then your bow?

APOLLO My custom is ever to carry it.

DEATH Yes! And you use it unjustly to aid this house!

APOLLO I grieve for a friend's woe.

DEATH So you would rob me of a second body?

APOLLO Not by force I won the other.

DEATH Why, then, is he in the world and not below the ground?

APOLLO In his stead he gives his wife-whom you have come to take.

DEATH And shall take-to the Underworld below the earth!

APOLLO Take her, and go! I know not if I can persuade you...

DEATH Not to kill her I must kill? I am appointed to that task.

APOLLO No, no! But to delay death for those about to die.

DEATH I hear your words and guess your wish!

APOLLO May not Alcestis live to old age?

DEATH No! I also prize my rights!

APOLLO Yet at most you win one life.

DEATH They who die young yield me a greater prize.

APOLLO If she dies old, the burial will be richer.

DEATH Phoebus, that argument favours the rich.

APOLLO What! Are you witty unawares?

DEATH The rich would gladly pay to die old.

APOLLO So you will not grant me this favour?

DEATH Not I! You know my nature.

APOLLO Yes! Hateful to men and a horror to the gods!

DEATH You cannot always have more than your due.

APOLLO Yet you shall change, most cruel though you are! For a man comes to the dwelling of Pheres, sent by Eurystheus to fetch a horse-drawn chariot from the harsh-wintered lands of Thrace; and he shall be a guest in the house of Admetus, and by force shall he tear this woman from you. Thus shall you gain no thanks from us, and yet you shall do this thing-and my hatred be upon you (APOLLO goes out. DEATH gazes after him derisively.)

DEATH Talk all you will, you get no more of me! The woman shall go down to the dwelling of Hades. Now must I go to consecrate her for the sacrifice with this sword; for when once this blade has shorn the victim's hair, then he is sacred to the Lower Gods! (DEATH enters the Palace by the open main door. The CHORUS enters from the right. They are the Elders or Notables of the city, and, therefore move slowly, leaning upon their staffs.)

LEADER OF THE CHORUS (chanting) Why is there no sound outside the Palace? Why is the dwelling of Admetus silent? Not a friend here to tell me if I must weep for a dead Queen or whether she lives and looks upon the light, Alcestis, the daughter of Pelias, whom among all women I hold the best wife to her spouse!

CHORUS (Singing) Is a sob to be heard? Or the beating of hands In the house? The lament for her end? Not one, Not one of her servants Stands at the gate!

Ah! to roll back the wave of our woe, O Healer, Appear!

FIRST SEMI-CHORUS Were she dead They had not been silent.

SECOND SEMI-CHORUS She is but a dead body!

FIRST SEMI-CHORUS Yet she has not departed the house.

SECOND SEMI-CHORUS Ah! Let me not boast! Why do you cling to hope?

FIRST SEMI-CHORUS Would Admetus bury her solitary, Make a grave alone for a wife so dear?

CHORUS At the gate I see not The lustral water from

the spring Which stands at the gates of the dead! No shorn tress in the portal Laid in lament for the dead! The young women beat not their hands!

SECOND SEMI-CHORUS Yet to-day is the day appointed....

FIRST SEMI-CHORUS Ah! What have you said?

SECOND SEMI-CHORUS When she must descend under earth

FIRST SEMI-CHORUS You have pierced my soul! You have pierced my mind!

SECOND SEMI-CHORUS He that for long Has been held in esteem Must weep when the good are destroyed.

CHORUS No! There is no place on earth To send forth a suppliant ship- Not to Lycia, Not to Ammon's waterless shrine- To save her from death! The dreadful doom is at hand. To what laden altar of what God Shall I turn my steps?

He alone- If the light yet shone for his eye- Asclepius, Phoebus's son, Could have led her back From the land of shadows, From the gates of Hades, For he raised the dead Ere the Zeus-driven shaft Slew him with thunder fire.... But now What hope can I hold for her life?

LEADER (chanting) The King has fulfilled Every rite; The altars of all the Gods Drip with the blood of slain beasts: Nothing, nothing avails. (From the women's quarters in the left wing of the Palace comes a woman in tears. She is not a slave, but one of the personal attendants on the Queen.) But now from the house comes one of her women servants, all in tears. What now shall I learn? (To the weeping Servant) It is well to weep when our lords are in sorrow-but tell us, we would know, is she alive, is she dead?

SERVANT You may say she is both alive and dead.

LEADER How can the same man be dead and yet behold

the light?

SERVANT She gasps, she is on the verge of death.

LEADER Ah, unhappy man! For such a husband what loss is such a wife!

SERVANT The King will not know his loss until he suffers it.

LEADER Then there is no hope that her life may be saved?

SERVANT The fated day constrains her.

LEADER Are all things befitting prepared for her?

SERVANT The robes in which her lord will bury her are ready.

LEADER Then let her know that she dies gloriously, the best of women beneath the sun by far!

SERVANT How should she not be the best! Who shall deny it? What should the best among women be? How better might a woman hold faith to her lord than gladly to die for him? This the whole city knows, but you will marvel when you hear what she has done within the house. When she knew that the last of her days was come she bathed her white body in river water, she took garments and gems from her rooms of cedar wood, and clad herself nobly; then, standing before the hearth-shrine, she uttered this prayer:

'O Goddess, since now I must descend beneath the earth, for the last time I make supplication to you: and entreat you to protect my motherless children. Wed my son to a fair bride, and my daughter to a noble husband. Let not my children die untimely, as I their mother am destroyed, but grant that they live out happy lives with good fortune in their own land!'

To every altar in Admetus's house she went, hung them with garlands. offered prayer, cut myrtle boughs-unweeping, unlamenting; nor did the coming doom change the bright colour of her face.

Then to her marriage-room she went, flung herself down upon her bed, and wept, and said:

'O my marriage-bed, wherein I loosed my virgin girdle to him for whom I die! Farewell! I have no hatred for you. Only me you lose. Because I held my faith to you and to my lord-I must die. Another woman shall possess you, not more chaste indeed than I, more fortunate perhaps.'

She fell upon her knees and kissed it, and all the bed was damp with the, tide of tears which flooded to her eyes. And when she was fulfilled of many tears, drooping she rose from her bed and made as if to go, and many times she turned to go and many times turned back, and flung herself once more upon the bed.

Her children clung to their mother's dress, and wept; and she clasped them in her arms and kissed them turn by turn, as a dying woman.

All the servants in the house wept with compassion for their Queen, But she held out her hand to each, and there was none so base to whom she did not speak, and who did not reply again.

Such is the misery in Admetus's house. If he had died, he would be nothing now; and, having escaped, he suffers an agony he will never forget.

LEADER And does Admetus lament this woe-since he must be robbed of so noble a woman?

SERVANT He weeps, and clasps in his arms his dear bed-fellow, and cries to her not to abandon him, asking impossible things. For she pines, and is wasted by sickness. She falls away, a frail burden on his arm; and yet, though faintly, she still breathes, still strives to look upon the sunlight, which she shall never see hereafter-since now for the last time she looks upon the orb and splendour of the sun I

I go, and shall announce that you are here; for all men

are not so well-minded to their lords as loyally to stand near them in misfortunes, but you for long have been a friend to both my lords. (She goes back into the women's quarters of the Palace. The CHORUS now begins to sing.)

FIRST SEMI-CHORUS O Zeus, What end to these woes? What escape from the Fate Which oppresses our lords?

SECOND SEMI-CHORUS Will none come forth? Must I shear my hair? Must we wrap ourselves In black mourning folds?

FIRST SEMI-CHORUS It is certain, O friends, it is certain?

But still let us cry to the Gods; Very great is the power of the Gods.

CHORUS O King, O Healer, Seek out appeasement To Admetus's agony! Grant this, Oh, grant it! Once before did you find it; Now once more Be the Releaser from death. The Restrainer of blood-drenched Hades!

SECOND SEMI-CHORUS Alas! O son of Pheres. What ills shall you suffer Being robbed of your spouse!

FIRST SEMI-CHORUS At sight of such woes Shall we cut our throats? Shall we slip A dangling noose round our necks?

CHORUS See! See! She comes From the house with her lord! Cry out, Oh, lament. O land of Pherae, For the best of women Fades away in her doom Under the earth, To dark Hades! (From the central door of the Palace comes a splendid but tragical procession. Preceded by the royal guards, ADMETUS enters, supporting ALCESTIS. The two children, a boy and a girl, cling to their mother's dress. There is a train of attendants and waiting women, who bring a low throne for the fainting ALCESTIS.)

LEADER OF THE CHORUS (chanting)'Never shall I say that we ought to rejoice in marriage, but rather weep; this have I seen from of old and now I look upon the fate of the King, who loses the best of wives, and henceforth until the end his life shall be intolerable.

ALCESTIS (chanting) Sun, and you, light of day, Vast whirlings of swift cloud!

ADMETUS The sun looks upon you and me, both of us miserable, who have wrought nothing against the Gods to deserve death.

ALCESTIS (chanting) O Earth, O roof-tree of my home, Bridal-bed of my country, Iolcus!

ADMETUS Rouse up, O unhappy one, and, do not leave me! Call upon the mighty Gods to pity!

ALCESTIS (starting up and gazing wildly in terror, chanting) I see the two-oared boat, I see the boat on the lake! And Charon, Ferryman of the Dead, Calls to me, his hand on the oar: 'Why linger? Hasten! You delay me!' Angrily he urges me.

ADMETUS Alas! How bitter to me is that ferrying of which you speak! O my unhappy one, how we suffer!

ALCESTIS (chanting) He drags me, he drags me away- Do you not see?- To the House of the Dead, The Winged One Glaring under dark brows, Hades!- What is it you do? Set me free!- What a path must I travel, O most hapless of women!

ADMETUS O piteous to those that love you, above all to me and to these children who sorrow in this common grief!

ALCESTIS (chanting) Loose me, Oh, loose me now; Lay me down; All strength is gone from my feet. (She falls back in the throne.) Hades draws near! Dark night falls on my eyes, My children, my children, Never more, Oh, never more Shall your mother be yours! O children, farewell, Live happy in the light of day!

ADMETUS (chanting) Alas! I hear this unhappy speech, and for me it is worse than all death. Ah! By the Gods, do not abandon me! Ah! By our children, whom you leave mother-less, take heart! If you die, I become as nothing; in you we have our life and death; we revere your love.

ALCESTIS   (recovering herself) Admetus, you see the things I suffer; and now before I die I mean to tell you what I wish.

To show you honour and-at the cost of my life-that you may still behold the light, I die; and yet I might have lived and wedded any in Thessaly I chose, and dwelt with happiness in a royal home. But, torn from you, I would not live with fatherless children, nor have I hoarded up those gifts of youth in which I found delight. Yet he who begot you, she who brought you forth, abandoned you when it had been beautiful in them to die, beautiful to die with dignity to save their son! They had no child but you, no hope if you were dead that other children might be born to them. Thus I should have lived my life out, and you too, and you would not lament as now, made solitary from your wife, that you must rear our children motherless!

But these things are a God's doing and are thus. Well! Do not forget this gift, for I shall ask-not a recompense, since nothing is more precious than life, but-only what is just, as you yourself will say, since if you have not lost your senses you must love these children no less than I. Let them be masters in my house; marry not again, and set a stepmother over them, a woman harsher than I, who in her jealousy will lift her hand against my children and yours. Ah! not this, let not this be, I entreat you! The new stepmother hates the first wife's children, the viper itself is not more cruel. The son indeed finds a strong rampart in his father-but you, my daughter, how shall you live your virgin life out in happiness? How will you fare with your father's new wife? Ah! Let her not cast evil report upon you and thus wreck your marriage in the height of your youth! You will have no mother, O my child, to give you in marriage, to comfort you in childbed when none is tenderer than a mother!

And I must die. Not to-morrow. nor to-morrow's morrow

comes this misfortune on me, but even now I shall be named with those that are no more. Farewell! Live happy! You, my husband, may boast you had the best of wives; and you, my children, that you lost the best of mothers! (She falls back.)

LEADER Take heart! I do not hesitate to speak for him. This he will do, unless he has lost his senses.

ADMETUS It shall be so, it shall be! Have no fear! And since I held you living as my wife, so, when dead, you only shall be called my wife, and in your place no bride of Thessaly shall salute me hers; no other woman is noble enough for that, no other indeed so beautiful of face. My children shall suffice me; I pray the Gods I may enjoy them, since you we have not enjoyed.

I shall wear mourning for you, O my wife, not for one year but all my days, abhorring the woman who bore me, hating my father-for they loved me in words, not deeds. But you-to save my life you give the dearest thing you have! Should I not weep then, losing such a wife as you?

I shall make an end of merry drinking parties, and of flower-crowned feasts and of the music which possessed my house. Never again shall I touch the lyre, never again shall I raise my spirits to sing to the Libyan flute-for you have taken from me all my joy. Your image, carven by the skilled hands of artists, shall be laid in our marriage-bed; I shall clasp it, and my hands shall cling to it and I shall speak your name and so, not having you, shall think I have my dear wife in my arms-a cold delight, I know, but it will lighten the burden of my days. Often you will gladden me, appearing in my dreams; for sweet it is to look on those we love in dreams, however brief the night.

Ah! If I had the tongue and song of Orpheus so that I might charm Demeter's Daughter or her Lord, and snatch you back from Hades, would go down to hell; and neither Pluto's dog nor Charon, Leader of the Dead, should hinder me until I had brought your life back to the light!

At least await me there whenever I shall die, and prepare

the house where you will dwell with me. I shall lay a solemn charge upon these children to stretch me in the same cedar shroud with you, and lay my side against your side; for even in death let me not be separate from you, you who alone were faithful to me!

LEADER (to ADMETUS) And I also will keep this sad mourning with you, as a friend with a friend; for she is worthy of it.

ALCESTIS O my children, you have heard your father say that never will he set another wife over you and never thus insult me.

ADMETUS Again I say it, and will perform it too!

ALCESTIS (placing the children's hands in his) Then take these children from my hand.

ADMETUS I take them-dear gifts from a dear hand.

ALCESTIS Now you must be the mother for me to my children.

ADMETUS It must be so, since they are robbed of you.

ALCESTIS O children, I should have lived my life out-and I go to the Underworld.

ADMETUS Alas! What shall I do, left alone by you?

ALCESTIS Time will console you. The dead are nothing.

ADMETUS Take me with you, by the Gods! Take me to the Underworld!

ALCESTIS It is enough that I should die-for you.

ADMETUS O Fate, what a wife you steal from me!

ALCESTIS (growing faint) My dimmed eyes are heavily oppressed.

ADMETUS O woman, I am lost if you leave me!

ALCESTIS You may say of me that I am nothing.

ADMETUS Lift up your head! Do not abandon your children!

ALCESTIS Ah! Indeed it is unwillingly-but, farewell, my children!

ADMETUS Look at them, look....

ALCESTIS I am nothing.

ADMETUS What are you doing? Are you leaving me?

ALCESTIS (falling back dead) Farewell.

ADMETUS (staring at the body) Wretch that I am, I am lost!

LEADER She is gone! The wife of Admetus is no more.

EUMELUS (chanting) Ah! Misery! Mother has gone, Gone to the Underworld! She lives no more, O my Father, In the sunlight. O sad one, You have left us To live motherless!

See, Oh, see her eyelids And her drooping hands! Mother, Mother, Hearken to me, listen, I beseech you! I-I-Mother!- I am calling to you, Your little bird fallen upon your face!

ADMETUS She hears not, she sees not. You and I are smitten by a dread calamity.

EUMELUS (chanting) Father, I am a child, And I am left Like a lonely ship By the mother I loved. Oh! The cruel things I suffer! And you, little sister, Suffer with me.

O my Father, Vain, vain was your wedding, You did not walk with her To the end of old age. She died first; And your death, O Mother, Destroys our house.

LEADER Admetus, you must endure this calamity. You are not the first and will not be the last to lose a noble wife. We all are doomed to die.

ADMETUS I know it. Not unawares did this woe swoop down on me; for long it has gnawed at me.

But, since I shall ordain the funeral rites for this dead body, you must be there, and meanwhile let a threnody re-echo to the implacable God of the Underworld. And all you men of Thessaly whom I rule-I order you to share the mourning for this woman with severed hair and black-robed garb. You who yoke the four-horsed chariot and the swift single horses, cut the mane from their necks with your steel.

Let there be no noise of flutes or lyre within the city until twelve moons are fulfilled. Never shall I bury another body so dear to me, never one that has loved me better. From me she deserves all honour, since she alone would die for me! (The body of ALCESTIS is carried solemnly into the Palace, followed by ADMETUS, With bowed head, holding one of his children by each hand. When all have entered, the great doors are quietly shut.)

CHORUS (singing, strophe 1)

O Daughter of Pelias, Hail to you in the house of Hades, In the sunless home where you shall dwell! Let Hades, the dark-haired God, Let the old man, Leader of the Dead, Who sits at the oar and helm, Know you: Far, far off is the best of women Borne beyond the flood of Acheron In the two-oared boat!

(antistrophe 1)

Often shall the Muses' servants Sing of you to the seven-toned Lyre-shell of the mountain-tortoise, And praise you with mourning songs at Sparta When the circling season Brings back the month Carneius Under the nightlong up-raised moon, And in bright glad Athens. Such a theme do you leave by your death For the music of singers!

(strophe 2)

Ah! That I had the power To bring you back to the light From the dark halls of Hades, And from the waves of Cocytus With the oar of the river of hell Oh, you only, O dearest of women, You only dared give your life For the life of your lord in Hades! Light rest the earth above you, O woman. If

your lord choose another bridal-bed He shall be hateful to
me As to your own children.

(antistrophe 2)

When his mother And the old father that begot him
Would not give their bodies to the earth For their son's sake,
They dared not deliver him-O cruel! Though their heads
were grey. But you, In your lively youth, Died for him, and
are gone from the light! Ah! might I be joined With a wife
so dear! But in life such fortune is rare. How happy were
my days with her! (From the left HERACLES enters. He
is black-bearded and of great physical strength; he wears a
lion-skin over his shoulders and carries a large club.)

HERACLES (with a gesture of salutation) Friends, dwell-
ers in the lands of Pherae, do I find Admetus in his home?

LEADER OF THE CHORUS The son of Pheres is in his
home, O Heracles. But, tell us, what brings you to the land of
Thessaly and to the city of Pherae?

HERACLES I have a task I must achieve for Eurystheus
of Tiryns.

LEADER Where do you go? To what quest are you
yoked?

HERACLES The quest of the four-horsed chariot of Di-
omedes, the Thracian.

LEADER But how will you achieve it? Do you know this
stranger?

HERACLES No, I have never been to the land of the Bistones.

LEADER You cannot obtain the horses without a struggle.

HERACLES I cannot renounce my labours.

LEADER You must kill to return, or you will remain
there dead.

HERACLES It will not be the first contest I have risked.

LEADER And if you conquer the King will you gain anything?

HERACLES I shall bring back his foals to the lord of Tiryns.

LEADER It is not easy to thrust the bit into their jaws.

HERACLES Only if they breathe fire from their nostrils!

LEADER But they tear men with their swift jaws.

HERACLES You speak of the food of wild mountain beasts, not of horses.

LEADER You may see their mangers foul with blood.

HERACLES Of what father does the breeder boast himself the son?

LEADER Of Ares, the lord of the gold-rich shield of Thrace!

HERACLES In this task once more you remind me of my fate, which is ever upon harsh steep ways, since I must join battle with the sons of Ares-first with Lycaon, then with Cycnus, and now in this third contest I am come to match myself with these steeds and their master!

LEADER But see, the lord of this land, Admetus himself, comes from the house! (The central doors of the Palace have opened, and ADMETUS comes slowly on the Stage, preceded and followed by guards and attendants. The King has put off all symbols of royalty, and is dressed in black. His tong hair is clipped close to his head. ADMETUS dissembles his grief throughout this scene, in obedience to the laws of hospitality, which were particularly reverenced in Thessaly.)

ADMETUS Hail Son of Zeus and of the blood of Perseus!

HERACLES And hail to you, Admetus, lord of the Thessalians

ADMETUS May it be so! I know your friendship well.

HERACLES What means this shorn hair, this mourning robe?

ADMETUS To-day I must bury a dead body.

HERACLES May a God avert harm from your children!

ADMETUS The children I have begotten are alive in the house.

HERACLES Your father was ripe for death-if it is he has gone?

ADMETUS He lives-and she who brought me forth, O Heracles.

HERACLES Your wife-Alcestis-she is not dead?

ADMETUS (evasively) Of her I might make a double answer.

HERACLES Do you mean that she is dead or alive?

ADMETUS (ambiguously) She is and is not-and for this I grieve.

HERACLES (perplexed) I am no wiser-you speak obscurely.

ADMETUS Did you not know the fate which must befall her?

HERACLES I know she submitted to die for you.

ADMETUS How then can she be alive, having consented to this?

HERACLES Ah! Do not weep for your wife till that time comes.

ADMETUS Those who are about to die are dead, and the dead are nothing.

HERACLES Men hold that to be and not to be are different things.

ADMETUS You hold for one, Heracles, and I for the other.

HERACLES Whom, then, do you mourn? Which of your friends is dead?

ADMETUS A woman. We spoke of her just now.

HERACLES (mistaking his meaning) A stranger? Or one born of your kin?

ADMETUS A stranger, but one related to this house.

HERACLES But how, then, did she chance to die in your house?

ADMETUS When her father died she was sheltered here.

HERACLES Alas! Would I had not found you in this grief, Admetus!

ADMETUS What plan are you weaving with those words?

HERACLES I shall go to the hearth of another friend.

ADMETUS Not so, O King! This wrong must not be.

HERACLES (hesitating) The coming of a guest is troublesome to those who mourn.

ADMETUS (decisively) The dead are dead. Enter my house.

HERACLES But it is shameful to feast among weeping friends.

ADMETUS We shall put you in the guest-rooms, which are far apart.

HERACLES Let me go, and I will give you a thousand thanks.

ADMETUS No, you shall not go to another man's hearth. (To a servant) Guide him, and open for him the guest-rooms apart from the house. (HERACLES enters the Palace by the guests' door; when he has gone in, ADMETUS turns to the other servants) Close the inner door of the courtyard; it is unseemly that guests rejoicing at table should hear lamentations, and be saddened. (The attendants go into the Palace.)

LEADER What are you about? When such a calamity has fallen upon you, Admetus, have you the heart to entertain a guest? Are you mad?

ADMETUS And if I had driven away a guest who came to my house and city, would you have praised me more? No, indeed! My misfortune would have been no less, and I inhospitable. One more ill would have been added to those I have if my house were called inhospitable. I myself find him the best of hosts when I enter the thirsty land of Argos.

LEADER But why did you hide from him the fate that has befallen, if the man came as a friend, as you say?

ADMETUS Never would he have entered my house if he had guessed my misfortune.

To some, I know, I shall appear senseless in doing this, and they will blame me; but my roof knows not to reject or insult a guest. (He goes into the Palace, as the CHORUS begins its song.)

CHORUS (singing, strophe 1)

O house of a bountiful lord, Ever open to many guests, The God of Pytho, Apollo of the beautiful lyre, Deigned to dwell in you And to live a shepherd in your lands! On the slope of the hillsides He played melodies of mating On the Pipes of Pan to his herds.

(antistrophe 1)

And the dappled lynxes fed with them In joy at your singing; From the wooded vale of Orthrys Came a yellow troop of lions; To the sound of your lyre, O Phoebus, Danced the dappled fawn Moving on light feet Beyond the high-crested pines, Charmed by your sweet singing.

(strophe 2)

He dwells in a home most rich in flocks By the lovely moving Boebian lake. At the dark stabling-place of the Sun He takes the sky of the Molossians As a bourne to his ploughing of fields, To the soils of his plains; He bears sway As far as the harbourless Coast of the Aegean Sea, As far as Pelion.

(antistrophe 2)

Even to-day he opened his house And received a guest, Though his eyelids were wet With tears wept by the corpse Of a dear bedfellow dead in the house. For the noble spirit is proclaimed by honour; All wisdom lies with the good. I admire him: And in my soul I know The devout man shall have joy. (The funeral procession of ALCESTIS enters from the door of the women's quarters. The body, carried on a bier by men servants, is followed by ADMETUS and his two children. Behind them comes a train of attendants and servants carrying the funeral offerings. All are in mourning. ADMETUS addresses the CHORUS.)

ADMETUS O friendly presence of you men of Pherae! Now that the body is prepared, and the servants bear it on high to the tomb and the fire, do you, as is fitting, salute the dead as she goes forth on her last journey. (PHERES, the father of ADMETUS, enters, followed by attendants bearing funeral offerings.)

LEADER OF THE CHORUS But I see your father, tottering with an old man's walk, and his followers bearing in their hands for your wife garments as an offering to the dead.

PHERES My son, I have come to share your sorrow, for the wife you have lost was indeed noble and virtuous-none can deny it. But these things must be endured, however intolerable they may be.

Take these garments, and let her descend under the

earth. Her body must be honoured, for she died to save your life, my son; she has not made me childless, nor left me to be destroyed without you in my hapless old age; and she has given glorious fame to all women by daring so noble a deed! (He lifts his hand in salutation to the body of ALCESTIS.) O woman, who saved my son, who raised me up when I had fallen, hail! Be happy in the halls of Hades! I declare it-such marriages are profitable to mankind; otherwise, it is foolish to marry.

ADMETUS (furiously) It was not my wish that you should come to this burial, and I deny that your presence is that of a friend! She shall never wear these garments of yours; she needs not your gifts for her burial. You should have grieved when I was, about to die; but you stood aside, and now do you come to wail over a corpse when you, an old man, allowed a young woman to die?

Were you in very truth father of this body of mine? Did she, who claims to be and is called my mother, bring me forth? Or was I bred of a slave's seed and secretly brought to your wife's breast? You have proved what you are when it comes to the test, and therefore I am not your begotten son; or you surpass all men in cowardice, for, being at the very verge and end of life, you had neither courage nor will to die for your son. But this you left to a woman, a stranger, whom alone I hold as my father and my mother!

Yet it had been a beautiful deed in you to die for your son, and short indeed was the time left you to live. She and I would have lived out our lives, and I should not now be here alone lamenting my misery.

You enjoyed all that a happy man can enjoy-you passed the flower of your age as a king, and in me your son you had an heir to your dominion; you would not have died childless, leaving an orphaned house to be plundered by strangers. You will not say that you abandoned me to death because I dishonoured your old age, for above all I was respectful to you-and this is the gratitude I have from you and my mother!

Beget more sons, and quickly, to cherish your old age and wrap you in a shroud when dead and lay your body out in state! This hand of mine shall not inter you. I am dead to you. I look upon the light of day because another saved me-I say I am her son, and will cherish her old age!

Vainly do old men pray for death, regretting their age and the long span of life. If death draws near, none wants to die, and age is no more a burden to him.

LEADER Admetus! The present misfortune is enough. Do not provoke your father's spirit. (ADMETUS turns angrily to depart, but PHERES prevents him.)

PHERES My son, do you think you are pursuing some hireling Lydian or Phrygian with your taunts? Do you know I am a Thessalian, a free man lawfully begotten by a Thessalian father? You are over-insolent, and you shall not leave thus, after wounding me with your boyish insults. I indeed begot you, and bred you up to be lord of this land, but I am not bound to die for you. It is not a law of our ancestors or of Hellas that the fathers should die for the children! You were born to live your own life, whether miserable or fortunate; and what is due to you from me you have. You rule over many men, and I shall leave you many wide fields even as received them from my own father. How, then, have I wronged you? Of what have I robbed you? Do not die for me, any more than I die for you. You love to look upon the light of day-do you think your father hates it? I tell myself that we are a long time underground and that life is short, but sweet.

But you-you strove shamelessly not to die, and you are alive, you shirked your fate by killing her! And you call me a coward, you, the worst of cowards, surpassed by a woman who died for you, pretty boy? And now you insult those who should be dear to you, when they refuse to die for a coward like you!

Be silent! Learn that if you love your life, so do others. If you utter insults, you shall hear many, and true ones too!

LEADER These insults and those that went before suffice. Old man, cease to revile your son.

ADMETUS (to PHERES) Speak on! I shall refute you. If the truth wounds you when you hear it you should not have wronged me.

PHERES I should have wronged you far more if I had died for you.

ADMETUS It is the same then to die an old man and in the flower of life?

PHERES We should live one life, not two.

ADMETUS May you live longer than God!

PHERES Do you curse your parents when they have done you no wrong?

ADMETUS I see you are in love with long life.

PHERES But you are not carrying her dead body in place of your own?

ADMETUS It is the proof of your cowardice, O worst of men.

PHERES You cannot say she died for me!

ADMETUS Alas! May you one day need my help.

PHERES Woo many women, so that more may die for you.

ADMETUS To your shame be it-you who dared not die.

PHERES Sweet is the daylight of the Gods, very sweet.

ADMETUS Your spirit is mean, not a man's.

PHERES Would you laugh to carry an old man's body to the grave?

ADMETUS You will die infamous, whenever you die.

PHERES It will matter little enough to me to hear ill of myself when I am dead!

ADMETUS Alas! Alas! full of impudence. is old age!

PHERES She was not impudent, but foolish,

ADMETUS Go! Leave me to bury her body.

PHERES (turning away) I go. You, her murderer, will bury her-but soon you must render an account to her relatives. Acastus is not a man if he fails to avenge his sister's blood on you! (PHERES goes out by the way he entered, followed by his attendants. ADMETUS gazes angrily after him.)

ADMETUS Go with a curse, you, and she who dwells with you! Grow old, as you ought, childless though you have a child. You shall never return to this house. And if I could renounce your hearth as my father's by heralds, I would do it. But we-since this sorrow must be endured-let us go, and set her body on the funeral pyre. (The Procession moves slowly along the stage, and is joined by the CHORUS. As they pass, the LEADER salutes the body of ALCESTIS.)

LEADER (chanting) Alas! Alas! You who suffer for your courage, O noblest and best of women, hail! May Hermes of the Dead, may Hades, greet you kindly. If there are rewards for the dead, may you share them as you sit by the bride of the Lord of the Dead! (The Procession has filed out. A servant in mourning hurries out from the guests' quarters.)

SERVANT Many guests from every land, I know, have come to the Palace of Admetus, and I have set food before them, but never one worse than this guest have I welcomed to the hearth.

First, though he saw our Lord was in mourning, he entered, and dared to pass through the gates. Then, knowing our misfortune, he did not soberly accept what was offered him, but if anything was not served to him he ordered us to bring it. In both hands he took a cup of ivy-wood, and drank the unmixed wine of the dark grape-mother, until he was encompassed and heated with the flame of wine. He crowned his head with myrtle sprays, howling discordant songs. There was he caring nothing for Admetus's misery, and we servants weeping for our Queen; and yet we hid our tear-laden eyes from the guest, for so Admetus had commanded.

And now in the Palace I must entertain this stranger, some villainous thief and brigand, while she, the Queen I mourn, has gone from the house unfollowed, unsaluted, she who was as a mother to me and all us servants, for she sheltered us from a myriad troubles by softening her husband's wrath.

Am I not right, then, to hate this stranger, who came to us in the midst of sorrow? (HERACLES comes from the Palace. He is drunkenly merry, with a myrtle wreath on his head, and a large cup and wine-skin in his hands. He staggers a little.)

HERACLES Hey, you! Why so solemn and anxious? A servant should not be sullen with guests, but greet them with a cheerful heart.

You see before you a man who is your lord's friend, and you greet him with a gloomy, frowning face, because of your zeal about a strange woman's death. Come here, and let me make you a little wiser! (With drunken gravity) Know the nature of human life? Don't think you do. You couldn't. Listen to me. All mortals must die. Isn't one who knows if he'll be alive to-morrow morning. Who knows where Fortune will lead? Nobody can teach it. Nobody learn it by rules. So, rejoice in what you hear, and learn from me! Count each day as it comes as Life-and leave the rest to Fortune. Above all, honour the Love Goddess, sweetest of all the Gods to mortal men, a kindly goddess! Put all the rest aside. Trust in what I say, if you think I speak truth-as I believe. Get rid of this gloom, rise superior to Fortune. Crown yourself with flowers and drink with me, won't you? I know the regular clink of the wine-cup will row you from darkness and gloom to another haven. Mortals should think mortal thoughts. To all solemn and frowning men, life I say is not life, but a disaster.

SERVANT We know all that, but what we endure here

to-day is far indeed from gladness and laughter.

HERACLES But the dead woman was a stranger. Lament not overmuch, then, for the Lords of this Palace are still alive.

SERVANT How, alive? Do you not know the misery of this house?

HERACLES Your lord did not lie to me?

SERVANT He goes too far in hospitality!

HERACLES But why should I suffer for a stranger's death?

SERVANT It touches this house only too nearly.

HERACLES Did he hide some misfortune from me?

SERVANT Go in peace! The miseries of our lords concern us.

HERACLES That speech does not imply mourning for a stranger!

SERVANT No, or I should not have been disgusted to see you drinking.

HERACLES Have I then been basely treated by my host?

SERVANT You did not come to this house at a welcome hour. We are in mourning. You see my head is shaved and the black garments I wear.

HERACLES But who, then, is dead? One of the children? The old father?

SERVANT O stranger, Admetus no longer has a wife.

HERACLES What! And yet I was received in this way?

SERVANT He was ashamed to send you away from his house.

HERACLES O hapless one! What a wife you have lost!

SERVANT Not she alone, but all of us are lost.

HERACLES (now completely sobered) I felt there was something when I saw his tear-wet eyes, his shaven head, his distracted look. But he persuaded me he was taking the body of a stranger to the grave. Against my will I entered these ates, and drank in the home of this generous man-and he in such grief! And shall I drink at such a time with garlands of flowers on my head? You, why did you not tell me that such misery had come upon this house? Where is he burying her? Where shall I find him?

SERVANT Beside the straight road which leads to Larissa you will see a tomb of polished stone outside the walls. (Returns to the servants' quarters)

HERACLES O heart of me, much-enduring heart, O right arm, now indeed must you show what son was born to Zeus by Alcmena, the Tirynthian, daughter of Electryon! For I must save this dead woman, and bring back Alcestis to this house as a grace to Admetus.

I shall watch for Death, the black-robed Lord of the Dead, and I know I shall find him near the tomb, drinking the blood of the sacrifices. If can leap upon him from an ambush, seize him, grasp him in my arms, no power in the world shall tear his bruised sides from me until he has yielded up this woman. If I miss my prey, if he does not come near the bleeding sacrifice, I will go down to Kore and her lord in their sunless dwelling, and I will make my entreaty to them, and I know they will give me Alcestis to bring back to the hands of the host who welcomed me, who did not repulse me from his house, though he was smitten with heavy woe which most nobly he hid from me! Where would be a warmer welcome in Thessaly or in all the dwellings of Hellas?

He shall not say he was generous to an ingrate! (HERACLES goes out. Presently ADMETUS and his attendants, followed by the CHORUS, return from the burial of ALCESTIS.)

ADMETUS (chanting) Alas! Hateful approach, hateful sight of my widowed house! Oh me! Oh me! Alas! Whither shall I go? Where rest? What can I say? What refrain from saying? Why can I not die? Indeed my mother bore me for a hapless fate. I envy the dead, I long to be with them, theirs are the dwellings where I would be. Without pleasure I look upon the light of day and set my feet upon the earth-so precious a hostage has Death taken from me to deliver unto Hades!

CHORUS (chanting responsively with ADMETUS) Go forward,

Enter your house.

ADMETUS Alas!

CHORUS Your grief deserves our tears.

ADMETUS O Gods!

CHORUS I know you have entered into sorrow.

ADMETUS Woe! Woe!

CHORUS Yet you bring no aid to the dead.

ADMETUS Oh me! Oh me!

CHORUS Heavy shall it be for you Never to look again On the face of the woman you love.

ADMETUS You bring to my mind the grief that breaks my heart. What sorrow is worse for a man than the loss of such a woman? I would I had never married, never shared my house with her. I envy the wifeless and the childless. They live but one life-what is suffering to them? But the sickness of children, bridal-beds ravished by Death-dreadful! when we might be wifeless and childless to the end.

CHORUS Chance, dreadful Chance, has stricken you.

ADMETUS Alas!

CHORUS But you set no limit to your grief.

ADMETUS Ah! Gods!

CHORUS A heavy burden to bear, and yet...

ADMETUS Woe! Woe!

CHORUS Courage! You are not the first to lose...

ADMETUS Oh me! Oh me!

CHORUS A wife. Different men Fate crushes with different blows.

ADMETUS O long grief and mourning for those beloved under the earth!

Why did you stay me from casting myself into the hollow grave to lie down for ever in death by the best of women? Two lives, not one, had then been seized by Hades, most faithful one to the other; and together we should have crossed the lake of the Underworld.

CHORUS A son most worthy of tears Was lost to one of my house, Yet, childless, he suffered with courage, Though the white was thick in his hair And his days were far-spent!

ADMETUS O visage of my house! How shall I enter you? How shall I dwell in you, now that Fate has turned its face from me? How great is the change! Once, of old, I entered my house with marriage-songs and the torches of Pelion, holding a loved woman by the hand, followed by a merry crowd shouting good wishes to her who is dead and to me, because we had joined our lives, being both noble and born of noble lines. Today, in place of marriage-songs are lamentations; instead of white garments I am clad in mourning, to return to my house and a solitary bed.

CHORUS Grief has fallen upon you In the midst of a happy life Untouched by misfortune. But your life and your spirit are safe. She is dead, She has left your love. Is this so new? Ere now many men Death has severed from wives.

ADMETUS (speaking) O friends, whatsoever may be thought by others, to me it seems that my wife's fate is happier than mine. Now, no pain ever shall touch her again; she has reached the noble end of all her sufferings. But I, I who should have died, I have escaped my fate, only to drag out a wretched life. Only now do I perceive it.

How shall I summon strength to enter this house? Whom shall I greet? Who will greet me in joy at my coming? Whither shall I turn my steps? I shall be driven forth by solitude when I see my bed widowed of my wife, empty the chairs on which she sat, a dusty floor beneath my roof, my children falling at my knees and calling for their mother, and the servants lamenting for the noble lady lost from the house!

Such will be my life within the house. Without, I shall be driven from marriage-feasts and gatherings of the women of Thessaly. I shall not endure to look upon my wife's friends. Those who hate me will say: 'See how he lives in shame, the man who dared not die, the coward who gave his wife to Hades in his stead! Is that a man? He hates his parents, yet he himself refused to die!'

This evil fame I have added to my other sorrows. O my friends, what then avails it that I live, if I must live in misery and shame? (He covers his head with his robe, and crouches in abject misery on the steps of his Palace.)

CHORUS (singing, strophe 1)

I have lived with the Muses And on lofty heights: Many doctrines have I learned; But Fate is above us all. Nothing avails against Fate Neither the Thracian tablets Marked with Orphic symbols, Nor the herbs given by Phoebus To the children of Asclepius To heal men of their sickness.

(antistrophe 1)

None can come near to her altars, None worship her statues; She regards not our sacrifice. O sacred goddess, Bear no more hardly upon me Than in days overpast! With a gesture Zeus judges, But the sentence is yours. Hard iron yields to your strength; Your fierce will knows not gentleness.

(strophe 2)

And the Goddess has bound you Ineluctably in the gyves of her hands. Yield. Can your tears give life to the dead? For the sons of the Gods Swoon in the shadow of Death. Dear was she in our midst, Dear still among the dead, For the noblest of women was she Who lay in your bed.

(antistrophe 2)

Ah! Let the grave of your spouse Be no more counted as a tomb, But revered as the Gods, And greeted by all who pass by! The wanderer shall turn from his path, Saying: 'She died for her lord; A blessed spirit she is now. Hail, O sacred lady, be our friend!' Thus shall men speak of her. (ADME-TUS is still crouched on the Palace steps, when HERACLES enters from the side, leading a veiled woman.)

LEADER OF THE CHORUS But see! The son of Alcmena, as I think, comes to your house. (ADMETUS uncovers his head, and faces the newcomer.)

HERACLES Admetus, a man should speak freely to his friends, and not keep reproaches silent in his heart. Since I was near you in your misfortune, should have wished to show myself your friend. But you did not tell me the dead body was your wife's, and you took me into your house as if you were in mourning only for a stranger. And I put a garland of flowers upon my head, and poured wine-offerings to the Gods, when your house was filled with lamentation. I blame you, yes, I blame you for this-but I will not upbraid you in your misfortune.

Why I turned back and am here, I shall tell you. Take and keep this woman for me until I have slain the King of the Bistones and return here with the horses of Thrace. If ill happens to me-may I return safely!-I give her to you to serve in your house.

With much striving I won her to my hands. On my way I found public games, worthy of athletes, and I have brought back this woman whom I won as the prize of victory. The winners of the easy tests had horses; heads of cattle were given to those who won in boxing and wrestling. Then came a woman as a prize. Since I was present, it would have been shameful for me to miss this glorious gain. Therefore, as I said, you must take care of this woman, whom I bring to you, not as one stolen but as the prize of my efforts. Perhaps in time you will approve of what I do.

ADMETUS Not from disdain, nor to treat you as a foe, did I conceal my wife's fate from you. But if you had turned aside to another man's hearth, one more grief had been added to my sorrow. It was enough that I should weep my woe.

This woman-O King, I beg it may be thus-enjoin some other Thessalian, one who is not in sorrow, to guard her. In Pherae there are many to welcome you. Do not remind me of my grief. Seeing her in my house, I could not restrain my tears. Add not a further anguish to my pain, for what I suffer is too great. And then-where could I harbour a young woman in my house? For she is young-I see by her clothes and jewels. Could she live with the men under my roof? How, then, could she remain chaste, if she moved to and fro among the young men? Heracles, it is not easy to restrain the young....I am thinking of your interests....Must I take her to my dead wife's room? How could I endure her to enter that bed? I fear a double reproach-from my people, who would accuse me of betraying my saviour to slip into another woman's bed, and from my dead wife, who deserves my respect, for which I must take care.

O woman, whosoever you may be, you have the form of Alcestis, and your body is like hers.

Ah! By all the Gods, take her from my sight! Do not insult a broken man. When I look upon her-she seems my wife-my heart is torn asunder-tears flow from my eyes. Miserable creature that I am, now taste the bitterness of my sorrow.

LEADER I do not praise this meeting; but, whatever happens, we must accept the gifts of the Gods.

HERACLES Oh, that I might bring your wife back into

the light of day from the dwelling of the Under-Gods, as a gift of grace to you!

ADMETUS I know you would wish this-but to what end? The dead cannot return to the light of day.

HERACLES Do not exaggerate, but bear this with decorum.

ADMETUS Easier to advise than bear the test.

HERACLES How will it aid you to lament for ever?

ADMETUS I know-but my love whirls me away.

HERACLES Love for the dead leads us to tears.

ADMETUS I am overwhelmed beyond words.

HERACLES You have lost a good wife-who denies it?

ADMETUS So that for me there is no more pleasure in life.

HERACLES Time will heal this open wound.

ADMETUS You might say Time, if Time were death!

HERACLES Another woman, a new marriage, shall console you.

ADMETUS Oh, hush! What have you said? A thing unbelievable!

HERACLES What! You will not marry? Your bed will remain widowed?

ADMETUS No other woman shall ever lie at my side.

HERACLES Do you think that avails the dead?

ADMETUS Wherever she may be, I must do her honour.

HERACLES I praise you-but men will call you mad.

ADMETUS Yet never more shall I be called a bridegroom.

HERACLES I praise your faithful love to your wife-

ADMETUS May I die if I betray her even when dead!

HERACLES (offering him the veiled woman's hand.) Receive her then into your noble house.

ADMETUS No, by Zeus who begot you, no!

HERACLES Yet you will do wrong if you do not take her.

ADMETUS If I do it, remorse will tear my heart.

HERACLES Yield-perhaps it will be a good thing for you.

ADMETUS Ah! If only you had not won her in the contest!

HERACLES But I conquered-and you conquered with me.

ADMETUS It is true-but let the woman go hence.

HERACLES She shall go, if she must. But first-ought she to go?

ADMETUS She must-unless it would anger you.

HERACLES There is good reason for my zeal.

ADMETUS You have conquered then-but not for my pleasure.

HERACLES One day you will praise me for it-be persuaded.

ADMETUS (to his attendants) Lead her in, since she must be received in this house.

HERACLES No, I cannot leave such a woman to servants.

ADMETUS Then lead her in yourself, if you wish.

HERACLES I must leave her in your hands.

ADMETUS I must not touch her-let her go into the house.

HERACLES I trust only in your right hand.

ADMETUS O King, you force me to this against my will.

HERACLES Put forth your hand and take this woman.

ADMETUS (turning aside his head) It is held out.

HERACLES As if you were cutting off a Gorgon's head! Do you hold her?

ADMETUS Yes.

HERACLES Then keep her. You shall not deny that the son of Zeus is a grateful guest. (Takes off the veil and shows ALCESTIS.) Look at her, and see if she is not like your wife. And may joy put an end to all your sorrow!

ADMETUS (drops her hand and starts back) O Gods! What am I to say? Unhoped-for wonder! Do I really look upon my wife? Or I am snared in the mockery of a God?

HERACLES No you look upon your wife indeed.

ADMETUS Beware! May it not be some phantom from the Underworld?

HERACLES Do not think your guest a sorcerer.

ADMETUS But do I indeed look upon the wife I buried?

HERACLES Yes-but I do not wonder at your mistrust.

ADMETUS Can I touch, speak to her, as my living wife?

HERACLES Speak to her-you have all you desired.

ADMETUS (taking ALCESTIS in his arms) O face and body of the dearest of women! I have you once more, when I thought I should never see you again!

HERACLES You have her-may the envy of the Gods be averted from you!

ADMETUS O noble son of greatest Zeus, fortune be yours, and may your Father guard you! But how did you bring her back from the Underworld to the light of day?

HERACLES By fighting with the spirit who was her master.

ADMETUS Then did you contend with Death?

HERACLES I hid by the tomb and leaped upon him.

ADMETUS But why is she speechless?

HERACLES You may not hear her voice until she is purified from her consecration to the Lower Gods, and until the third dawn has risen. Lead her in.

And you, Admetus, show as ever a good man's welcome to your guests.

Farewell! I go to fulfil the task set me by the King, the son of Sthenelus.

ADMETUS Stay with us, and share our hearth.

HERACLES That may be hereafter, but now I must be gone in haste. (HERACLES departs.)

ADMETUS (gazing after him) Good fortune to you, and come back here! (To the CHORUS) In all the city and in the four quarters of Thessaly let there be choruses to rejoice at this good fortune, and let the altars smoke with the flesh of oxen in sacrifice! To-day we have changed the past for a better life. I am happy. (He leads ALCESTIS into the Palace.)

CHORUS (singing) Spirits have many shapes, Many strange things are performed by the Gods. The expected does not always happen, And God makes a way for the unexpected. So ends this action.

THE END

MEDEA

Dramatis Personae

NURSE OF MEDEA
ATTENDANT ON HER CHILDREN
MEDEA
CHORUS OF CORINTHIAN WOMEN
CREON, King of Corinth
JASON
AEGEUS, King of Athens
MESSENGER

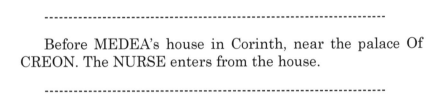

Before MEDEA's house in Corinth, near the palace Of CREON. The NURSE enters from the house.

NURSE Ah! Would to Heaven the good ship Argo ne'er had sped its course to the Colchian land through the misty blue Symplegades, nor ever in the glens of Pelion the pine been felled to furnish with oars the chieftain's hands, who went to fetch the golden fleece for Pelias; for then would my own mistress Medea never have sailed to the turrets of Iolcos, her soul with love for Jason smitten, nor would she have beguiled the daughters of Pelias to slay their father and come to live here in the land of Corinth with her husband and children, where her exile found favour with the citizens to whose land she had come, and in all things of her own accord was she at one with Jason, the greatest safeguard this when wife and husband do agree; but now their love is all turned to hate, and tenderest ties are weak. For Jason hath betrayed his own children and my mistress dear for the love of a royal bride, for he hath wedded the daughter of Creon, lord of this land. While Medea, his hapless wife, thus scorned, appeals to the oaths he swore, recalls the strong pledge his right hand gave, and bids heaven be witness what requital she is finding from Jason. And here she lies fasting, yielding her body to her grief, wasting away in tears ever since she learnt that she was wronged by her husband, never lifting her eye nor raising her face from off the ground; and she lends as deaf an ear to her friend's warning as if she were a rock or ocean billow, save when she turns her snow-white neck aside and softly to herself bemoans her father dear, her country and her home, which she gave up to come hither with the man who now holds her in dishonour. She, poor lady, hath by sad experience learnt how good a thing it is never to quit one's native land. And she hates her children now and feels no joy at seeing them; I fear she may contrive some untoward scheme; for her mood is dangerous nor will she brook her cruel treatment; full well I know her, and I much do dread that she will plunge the keen sword through their hearts, stealing without a word into the chamber where their marriage couch is spread, or else that she will slay the prince and bridegroom too, and so find some calamity still more grievous than the present; for dreadful is her wrath; verily the man that doth incur her hate will have no easy task to raise o'er her a song of triumph. Lo! where her sons come hither from their childish sports; little they reck of their mother's woes, for the soul of the young is no friend to sorrow. (The AT-TENDANT leads in MEDEA'S children.)

ATTENDANT Why dost thou, so long my lady's own handmaid, stand here at the gate alone, loudly lamenting to thyself the piteous tale? how comes it that Medea will have thee leave her to herself?

NURSE Old man, attendant on the sons of Jason, our masters' fortunes when they go awry make good slaves grieve and touch their hearts. Oh! have come to such a pitch of grief that there stole a yearning wish upon me to come forth hither and proclaim to heaven and earth my mistress's hard fate.

ATTENDANT What! has not the poor lady ceased yet

from her lamentation?

NURSE Would I were as thou art! the mischief is but now beginning; it has not reached its climax yet.

ATTENDANT O foolish one, if I may call my mistress such a name; how little she recks of evils yet more recent!

NURSE What mean'st, old man? grudge not to tell me.

ATTENDANT 'Tis naught; I do repent me even of the words I have spoken.

NURSE Nay, by thy beard I conjure thee, hide it not from thy fellow-slave; will be silent, if need be, on that text.

ATTENDANT I heard one say, pretending not to listen as I approached the place where our greybeards sit playing draughts near Pirene's sacred spring, that Creon, the ruler of this land, is bent on driving these children and their mother from the boundaries of Corinth; but I know not whether the news is to be relied upon, and would fain it were not.

NURSE What! will Jason brook such treatment of his sons, even though he be at variance with their mother?

ATTENDANT Old ties give way to new; he bears no longer any love to this family.

NURSE Undone, it seems, are we, if to old woes fresh ones we add, ere we have drained the former to the dregs.

ATTENDANT Hold thou thy peace, say not a word of this; 'tis no time for our mistress to learn hereof.

NURSE O children, do ye hear how your father feels towards you? Perdition catch him, but no he is my master still; yet is he proved a very traitor to his nearest and dearest.

ATTENDANT And who 'mongst men is not? Art learning only now, that every single man cares for himself more than for his neighbour, some from honest motives, others for mere gain's sake? seeing that to indulge his passion their father has ceased to love these children.

NURSE Go, children, within the house; all will be well. Do thou keep them as far away as may be, and bring them not near their mother in her evil hour. For ere this have I seen her eyeing them savagely, as though she were minded to do them some hurt, and well I know she will not cease from her fury till she have pounced on some victim. At least may she turn her hand against her foes, and not against her friends.

MEDEA (chanting within) Ah, me! a wretched suffering woman I! O would that I could die!

NURSE (chanting) 'Tis as I said, my dear children; wild fancies stir your mother's heart, wild fury goads her on. Into the house without delay, come not near her eye, approach her not, beware her savage mood, the fell tempest of her reckless heart. In, in with what speed ye may. For 'tis plain she will soon redouble her fury; that cry is but the herald of the gathering storm-cloud whose lightning soon will flash; what will her proud restless soul, in the anguish of despair, be guilty of? (The ATTENDANT takes the children into the house. MEDEA (chanting within) Ah, me! the agony I have suffered, deep enough to call for these laments! Curse you and your father too, ye children damned, sons of a doomed mother! Ruin seize the whole family!

NURSE (chanting) Ah me! ah me! the pity of it! Why, pray, do thy children share their father's crime? Why hatest thou them? Woe is you, poor children, how do I grieve for you lest ye suffer some outrage! Strange are the tempers of princes, and maybe because they seldom have to obey, and mostly lord it over others, change they their moods with difficulty. 'Tis better then to have been trained to live on equal terms. Be it mine to reach old age, not in proud pomp, but in security! Moderation wins the day first as a better word for men to use, and likewise it is far the best course for them to pursue; but greatness that doth o'erreach itself, brings no blessing to mortal men; but pays a penalty of greater ruin whenever fortune is wroth with a family. (The CHORUS enters. The following lines between the NURSE, CHORUS, and MEDEA are sung.)

CHORUS I heard the voice, uplifted loud, of our poor Colchian lady, nor yet is she quiet; speak, aged dame, for as I stood by the house with double gates I heard a voice of weeping from within, and I do grieve, lady, for the sorrows of this house, for it hath won my love.

NURSE 'Tis a house no more; all that is passed away long since; a royal bride keeps Jason at her side, while our mistress pines away in her bower, finding no comfort for her soul in aught her friends can say.

MEDEA (within) Oh, oh! Would that Heaven's levin bolt would cleave this head in twain! What gain is life to me? Woe, woe is me! O, to die and win release, quitting this loathed existence!

CHORUS Didst hear, O Zeus, thou earth, and thou, O light, the piteous note of woe the hapless wife is uttering? How shall a yearning for that insatiate resting-place ever hasten for thee, poor reckless one, the end that death alone can bring? Never pray for that. And if thy lord prefers a fresh love, be not angered with him for that; Zeus will judge 'twixt thee and him herein. Then mourn not for thy husband's loss too much, nor waste thyself away.

MEDEA (within) Great Themis, and husband of Themis, behold what I am suffering now, though I did bind that accursed one, my husband, by strong oaths to me! O, to see him and his bride some day brought to utter destruction, they and their house with them, for that they presume to wrong me thus unprovoked. O my father, my country, that I have left to my shame, after slaying my own brother.

NURSE Do ye hear her words, how loudly she adjures Themis, oft invoked, and Zeus, whom men regard as keeper of their oaths? On no mere trifle surely will our mistress spend her rage.

CHORUS Would that she would come forth for us to see, and listen to the words of counsel we might give, if haply she might lay aside the fierce fury of her wrath, and her temper stern. Never be my zeal at any rate denied my friends! But go thou and bring her hither outside the house, and tell her this our friendly thought; haste thee ere she do some mischief to those inside the house, for this sorrow of hers is mounting high.

NURSE This will I do; but I doubt whether I shall persuade my mistress; still willingly will I undertake this trouble for you; albeit, she glares upon her servants with the look of a lioness with cubs, whenso anyone draws nigh to speak to her. Wert thou to call the men of old time rude uncultured boors thou wouldst not err, seeing that they devised their hymns for festive occasions, for banquets, and to grace the board, a pleasure to catch the ear, shed o'er our life, but no man hath found a way to allay hated grief by music and the minstrel's varied strain, whence arise slaughters and fell strokes of fate to o'erthrow the homes of men. And yet this were surely a gain, to heal men's wounds by music's spell, but why tune they their idle song where rich banquets are spread? For of itself doth the rich banquet, set before them, afford to men delight.

CHORUS I heard a bitter cry of lamentation! loudly, bitterly she calls on the traitor of her marriage bed, her perfidious spouse; by grievous wrongs oppressed she invokes Themis, bride of Zeus, witness of oaths, who brought her unto Hellas, the land that fronts the strand of Asia, o'er the sea by night through ocean's boundless gate. (As the CHORUS finishes its song, MEDEA enters from the house.)

MEDEA From the house I have come forth, Corinthian ladies, for fear lest you be blaming me; for well I know that amongst men many by showing pride have gotten them an ill name and a reputation for indifference, both those who shun men's gaze and those who move amid the stranger crowd, and likewise they who choose a quiet walk in life. For there is no just discernment in the eyes of men, for they, or ever they have surely learnt their neighbour's heart, loathe him at first sight, though never wronged by him; and so a stranger most of all should adopt a city's views; nor do I commend that citizen, who, in the stubbornness of his heart, from churlishness resents the city's will.

But on me hath fallen this unforeseen disaster, and sapped my life; ruined I am, and long to resign the boon of existence, kind friends, and die. For he who was all the world to me, as well thou knowest, hath turned out the worst of men, my own husband. Of all things that have life and sense we women are the most hapless creatures; first must we buy a husband at a great price, and o'er ourselves a tyrant set which is an evil worse than the first; and herein lies the most important issue, whether our choice be good or bad. For divorce is not honourable to women, nor can we disown our lords. Next must the wife, coming as she does to ways and customs new, since she hath not learnt the lesson in her home, have a diviner's eye to see how best to treat the partner of her life. If haply we perform these tasks with thoroughness and tact, and the husband live with us, without resenting the yoke, our life is a happy one; if not, 'twere best to die. But when a man is vexed with what he finds indoors, he goeth forth and rids his soul of its disgust, betaking him to some friend or comrade of like age; whilst we must needs regard his single self.

And yet they say we live secure at home, while they are at the wars, with their sorry reasoning, for I would gladly take my stand in battle array three times o'er, than once give birth. But enough! this language suits not thee as it does me; thou hast a city here, a father's house, some joy in life, and friends to share thy thoughts, but I am destitute, without a city, and therefore scorned by my husband, a captive I from a foreign shore, with no mother, brother, or kinsman in whom to find a new haven of refuge from this calamity. Wherefore this one boon and only this I wish to win from thee,-thy silence, if haply I can some way or means devise to avenge me on my husband for this cruel treatment, and on the man who gave to him his daughter, and on her who is his wife. For though woman be timorous enough in all else, and as regards courage, a coward at the mere sight of steel, yet in the moment she finds her honour wronged, no heart is filled with deadlier thoughts than hers.

LEADER OF THE CHORUS This will I do; for thou wilt

be taking a just vengeance on thy husband, Medea. That thou shouldst mourn thy lot surprises me not. But lo! I see Creon, king of this land coming hither, to announce some new resolve. (CREON enters, with his retinue.)

CREON Hark thee, Medea, I bid thee take those sullen looks and angry thoughts against thy husband forth from this land in exile, and with thee take both thy children and that without delay, for I am judge in this sentence, and I will not return unto my house till I banish thee beyond the borders of the land.

MEDEA Ah, me! now is utter destruction come upon me, unhappy that I am! For my enemies are bearing down on me full sail, nor have I any landing-place to come at in my trouble. Yet for all my wretched plight I will ask thee, Creon, wherefore dost thou drive me from the land?

CREON I fear thee,-no longer need I veil my dread 'neath words,-lest thou devise against my child some cureless ill. Many things contribute to this fear of mine; thou art a witch by nature, expert in countless sorceries, and thou art chafing for the loss of thy husband's affection. I hear, too, so they tell me, that thou dost threaten the father of the bride, her husband, and herself with some mischief; wherefore I will take precautions ere our troubles come. For 'tis better for me to incur thy hatred now, lady, than to soften my heart and bitterly repent it hereafter.

MEDEA Alas! this is not now the first time, but oft before, O Creon, hath my reputation injured me and caused sore mischief. Wherefore whoso is wise in his generation ought never to have his children taught to be too clever; for besides the reputation they get for idleness, they purchase bitter odium from the citizens. For if thou shouldst import new learning amongst dullards, thou wilt be thought a useless trifler, void of knowledge; while if thy fame in the city o'ertops that of the pretenders to cunning knowledge, thou wilt win their dislike. I too myself share in this ill-luck. Some think me clever and hate me, others say I am too reserved, and some the very reverse; others find me hard to please and not so very clever after all. Be that as it may, thou dost fear me lest I bring on thee something to mar thy harmony. Fear me not, Creon, my position scarce is such that should seek to quarrel with princes. Why should I, for how hast thou injured me? Thou hast betrothed thy daughter where thy fancy prompted thee. No, 'tis my husband I hate, though I doubt not thou hast acted wisely herein. And now I grudge not thy prosperity; betroth thy child, good luck to thee, but let me abide in this land, for though I have been wronged I will be still and yield to my superiors.

CREON Thy words are soft to hear, but much I dread lest thou art devising some mischief in thy heart, and less than ever do I trust thee now; for cunning woman, and man likewise, is easier to guard against when quick-tempered than when taciturn. Nay, begone at once! speak me no speeches, for this is decreed, nor hast thou any art whereby thou shalt abide amongst us, since thou hatest me.

MEDEA O, say not so! by thy knees and by thy daughter newlywed, I do implore!

CREON Thou wastest words; thou wilt never persuade me.

MEDEA What, wilt thou banish me, and to my prayers no pity yield?

CREON I will, for I love not thee above my own family.

MEDEA O my country! what fond memories I have of thee in this hour!

CREON Yea, for I myself love my city best of all things save my children.

MEDEA Ah me! ah me! to mortal man how dread a scourge is love!

CREON That, I deem, is according to the turn our fortunes take.

MEDEA O Zeus! let not the author of these my troubles

escape thee.

CREON Begone, thou silly woman, and free me from my toil.

MEDEA The toil is mine, no lack of it.

CREON Soon wilt thou be thrust out forcibly by the hand of servants.

MEDEA Not that, not that, I do entreat thee, Creon

CREON Thou wilt cause disturbance yet, it seems.

MEDEA I will begone; I ask thee not this boon to grant.

CREON Why then this violence? why dost thou not depart?

MEDEA Suffer me to abide this single day and devise some plan for the manner of my exile, and means of living for my children, since their father cares not to provide his babes therewith. Then pity them; thou too hast children of thine own; thou needs must have a kindly heart. For my own lot I care naught, though I an exile am, but for those babes I weep, that they should learn what sorrow means.

CREON Mine is a nature anything but harsh; full oft by showing pity have suffered shipwreck; and now albeit I clearly see my error, yet shalt thou gain this request, lady; but I do forewarn thee, if tomorrow's rising sun shall find thee and thy children within the borders of this land, thou diest; my word is spoken and it will not lie. So now, if abide thou must, stay this one day only, for in it thou canst not do any of the fearful deeds I dread. (CREON and his retinue go out.)

CHORUS (chanting) Ah! poor lady, woe is thee! Alas, for thy sorrows! Whither wilt thou turn? What protection, what home or country to save thee from thy troubles wilt thou find? O Medea, in what a hopeless sea of misery heaven hath plunged thee!

MEDEA On all sides sorrow pens me in. Who shall gainsay this? But all is not yet lost! think not so. Still are there troubles in store for the new bride, and for her bridegroom no light toil. Dost think I would ever have fawned on yonder man, unless to gain some end or form some scheme? Nay, would not so much as have spoken to him or touched him with my hand. But he has in folly so far stepped in that, though he might have checked my plot by banishing me from the land, he hath allowed me to abide this day, in which I will lay low in death three of my enemies-a father and his daughter and my husband too. Now, though I have many ways to compass their death, I am not sure, friends, which I am to try first. Shall I set fire to the bridal mansion, or plunge the whetted sword through their hearts, softly stealing into the chamber where their couch is spread? One thing stands in my way. If I am caught making my way into the chamber, intent on my design, I shall be put to death and cause my foes to mock, 'Twere best to take the shortest way-the way we women are most skilled in-by poison to destroy them. Well, suppose them dead; what city will receive me? What friendly host will give me a shelter in his land, a home secure, and save my soul alive? None. So I will wait yet a little while in case some tower of defence rise up for me; then will I proceed to this bloody deed in crafty silence; but if some unexpected mischance drive me forth, I will with mine own hand seize the sword, e'en though I die for it, and slay them, and go forth on my bold path of daring. By that dread queen whom I revere before all others and have chosen to share my task, by Hecate who dwells within my inmost chamber, not one of them shall wound my heart and rue it not. Bitter and sad will I make their marriage for them; bitter shall be the wooing of it, bitter my exile from the land. Up, then, Medea, spare not the secrets of thy art in plotting and devising; on to the danger. Now comes a struggle needing courage. Dost see what thou art suffering? 'Tis not for thee to be a laughing-stock to the race of Sisyphus by reason of this wedding of Jason, sprung, as thou art, from noble sire, and of the Sun-god's race. Thou hast cunning; and, more than this, we women, though by nature little apt for virtuous deeds, are most expert to fashion any mischief.

CHORUS (singing, strophe 1)

Back to their source the holy rivers turn their tide. Order and the universe are being reversed. 'Tis men whose counsels are treacherous, whose oath by heaven is no longer sure. Rumour shall bring a change o'er my life, bringing it into good repute. Honour's dawn is breaking for woman's sex; no more shall the foul tongue of slander fix upon us.

(antistrophe 1)

The songs of the poets of old shall cease to make our faithlessness their theme. Phoebus, lord of minstrelsy, hath not implanted in our mind the gift of heavenly song, else had I sung an answering strain to the race of males, for time's long chapter affords many a theme on their sex as well as ours.

(strophe 2)

With mind distraught didst thou thy father's house desert on thy voyage betwixt ocean's twin rocks, and on a foreign strand thou dwellest thy bed left husbandless, poor lady, and thou an exile from the land, dishonoured, persecuted.

(antistrophe 2)

Gone is the grace that oaths once had. Through all the breadth of Hellas honour is found no more; to heaven hath it sped away. For thee no father's house is open, woe is thee! to be a haven from the troublous storm, while o'er thy home is set another queen, the bride that is preferred to thee. (As the CHORUS finishes its song, JASON enters, alone. MEDEA comes out of the house.)

JASON It is not now I first remark, but oft ere this, how unruly a pest is a harsh temper. For instance, thou, hadst thou but patiently endured the will of thy superiors, mightest have remained here in this land and house, but now for thy idle words wilt thou be banished. Thy words are naught to me. Cease not to call Jason basest of men; but for those words thou hast spoken against our rulers, count it all gain that exile is thy only punishment. I ever tried to check the outbursts of the angry monarch, and would have had thee stay, but thou wouldst not forego thy silly rage, always reviling our rulers, and so thou wilt be banished. Yet even after all this I weary not of my goodwill, but am come with thus much forethought, lady, that thou mayst not be destitute nor want for aught, when, with thy sons, thou art cast out. Many an evil doth exile bring in its train with it; for even though thou hatest me, never will I harbour hard thoughts of thee.

MEDEA Thou craven villain (for that is the only name my tongue can find for thee, a foul reproach on thy unmanliness), comest thou to me, thou, most hated foe of gods, of me, and of all mankind? 'Tis no proof of courage or hardihood to confront thy friends after injuring them, but that worst of all human diseases-loss of shame. Yet hast thou done well to come; for I shall ease my soul by reviling thee, and thou wilt be vexed at my recital. I will begin at the very beginning. I saved thy life, as every Hellene knows who sailed with thee aboard the good ship Argo, when thou wert sent to tame and yoke fire-breathing bulls, and to sow the deadly tilth. Yea, and I slew the dragon which guarded the golden fleece, keeping sleepless watch o'er it with many a wreathed coil, and I raised for thee a beacon of deliverance. Father and home of my free will I left and came with the to Iolcos, 'neath Pelion's hills, for my love was stronger than my prudence. Next I caused the death of Pelias by a doom most grievous, even by his own children's hand, beguiling them of all their fear. All this have I done for thee, thou traitor! and thou hast cast me over, taking to thyself another wife, though children have been born to us. Hadst thou been childless still, I could have pardoned thy desire for this new union. Gone is now the trust I put in oaths. I cannot even understand whether thou thinkest that the gods of old no longer rule, or that fresh decrees are now in vogue amongst mankind, for thy conscience must tell thee thou hast not kept faith with me. Ah! poor right hand, which thou didst often grasp. These knees thou didst embrace! All in vain, I suffered a traitor to touch me! How short of my hopes I am fallen! But come, I will deal with the as though thou wert my friend. Yet what kindness can I expect from one so base as thee? But yet I will do it, for my questioning will show thee yet more base. Whither can I turn me now? to my father's house, to my own country, which I for thee deserted to come hither? to the hapless daughters of Pelias? A glad welcome, I trow, would they give me in their home, whose father's death I compassed! My case stands even thus: I am become the bitter foe to those of mine own home, and those whom I need ne'er have wronged I have made mine enemies to pleasure thee. Wherefore to reward me for this thou hast made me doubly blest in the eyes of many wife in Hellas; and in thee I own a peerless, trusty lord. O woe is me, if indeed I am to be cast forth an exile from the land, without one friend; one lone woman with her babes forlorn! Yea, a fine reproach to thee in thy bridal hour, that thy children and the wife who saved thy life are beggars and vagabonds! O Zeus! why hast thou granted unto man clear signs to know the sham in gold, while on man's brow no brand is stamped whereby to gauge the villain's heart?

LEADER OF THE CHORUS There is a something terrible and past all cure, when quarrels arise 'twixt those who are near and dear.

JASON Needs must I now, it seems, turn orator, and, like a good helmsman on a ship with close-reefed sails, weather that wearisome tongue of thine. Now, I believe, since thou wilt exaggerate thy favours, that to Cypri, alone of gods or men I owe the safety of my voyage. Thou hast a subtle wit enough; yet were it a hateful thing for me to say that the Love-god constrained thee by his resistless shaft to save my life. However, I will not reckon this too nicely; 'twas kindly done, however thou didst serve me. Yet for my safety hast thou received more than ever thou gavest, as I will show. First, thou dwellest in Hellas, instead of thy barbarian land, and hast learnt what justice means and how to live by law, not by the dictates of brute force; and all the Hellenes recognize thy cleverness, and thou hast gained a name; whereas, if thou hadst dwelt upon the confines of the earth, no tongue had mentioned thee. Give me no gold within my halls, nor skill to sing a fairer strain than ever Orpheus sang, unless there-with my fame be spread abroad! So much I say to thee about my own toils, for 'twas thou didst challenge me to this retort. As for the taunts thou urgest against my marriage with the princess, I will prove to thee, first, that I am prudent herein, next chastened in my love, and last powerful friend to thee and to thy sons; only hold thy peace. Since I have here withdrawn from Iolcos with many a hopeless trouble at my back, what happier device could I, an exile, frame than marriage with the daughter of the king? 'Tis not because I loathe thee for my wife-the thought that rankles in thy heart; 'tis not because I am smitten with desire for a new bride, nor yet that I am eager to vie with others in begetting many children, for those we have are quite enough, and I do not complain. Nay, 'tis that we-and this is most important-may dwell in comfort, instead of suffering want (for well I know that every whilom friend avoids the poor) , and that I might rear my sons as doth befit my house; further, that I might be the father of brothers for the children thou hast borne, and raise these to the same high rank, uniting the family in one,-to my lasting bliss. Thou, indeed, hast no need of more children, but me it profits to help my present family by that which is to be. Have I miscarried here? Not even thou wouldest say so unless a rival's charms rankled in thy bosom. No, but you women have such strange ideas, that you think all is well so long as your married life runs smooth; but if some mischance occur to ruffle your love, all that was good and lovely erst you reckon as your foes. Yea, men should have begotten children from some other source, no female race existing; thus would no evil ever have fallen on mankind.

LEADER This speech, O Jason, hast thou with specious art arranged; but yet I think-albeit in speaking I am indiscreet-that thou hast sinned in thy betrayal of thy wife.

MEDEA No doubt I differ from the mass of men on many points; for, to my mind, whoso hath skill to fence with words in an unjust cause, incurs the heaviest penalty; for such an one, confident that he can cast a decent veil of words o'er his injustice, dares to practise it; and yet he is not so very clever after all. So do not thou put forth thy specious pleas and clever words to me now, for one word of mine will lay thee low. Hadst thou not had a villain's heart, thou shouldst have gained my consent, then made this match, instead of hiding it from those who loved thee.

JASON Thou wouldest have lent me ready aid, no doubt, in this proposal, if had told thee of my marriage, seeing that not even now canst thou restrain thy soul's hot fury.

MEDEA This was not what restrained thee; but thine eye was turned towards old age, and a foreign wife began to appear a shame to thee.

JASON Be well assured of this: 'twas not for the woman's sake I wedded the king's daughter, my present wife; but, as I have already told thee, I wished to insure thy safety and to be the father of royal sons bound by blood to my own children-a bulwark to our house.

MEDEA May that prosperity, whose end is woe, ne'er be mine, nor such wealth as would ever sting my heart!

JASON Change that prayer as I will teach thee, and thou wilt show more wisdom. Never let happiness appear in sorrow's guise, nor, when thy fortune smiles, pretend she frowns!

MEDEA Mock on; thou hast a place of refuge; I am alone, an exile soon to be.

JASON Thy own free choice was this; blame no one else.

MEDEA What did I do? Marry, then betray thee?

JASON Against the king thou didst invoke an impious curse.

MEDEA On thy house too maybe I bring the curse.

JASON Know this, I will no further dispute this point with thee. But, if thou wilt of my fortune somewhat take for the children or thyself to help thy exile, say on; for I am ready to grant it with ungrudging hand, yea and to bend tokens to my friends elsewhere who shall treat thee well. If thou refuse this offer, thou wilt do a foolish deed, but if thou cease from anger the greater will be thy gain.

MEDEA I will have naught to do with friends of thine, naught will I receive of thee, offer it not to me; a villain's gifts can bring no blessing.

JASON At least I call the gods to witness, that I am ready in all things to serve thee and thy children, but thou dost scorn my favours and thrustest thy friends stubbornly away; wherefore thy lot will be more bitter still.

MEDEA Away! By love for thy young bride entrapped, too long thou lingerest outside her chamber; go wed, for, if God will, thou shalt have such a marriage as thou wouldst fain refuse. (JASON goes out.)

CHORUS (singing, strophe 1)

When in excess and past all limits Love doth come, he brings not glory or repute to man; but if the Cyprian queen in moderate might approach, no goddess is so full of charm as she. Never, O never, lady mine, discharge at me from thy golden bow a shaft invincible, in passion's venom dipped.

(antistrophe 1)

On me may chastity, heaven's fairest gift, look with a favouring eye; never may Cypris, goddess dread, fasten on me a temper to dispute, or restless jealousy, smiting my soul with mad desire for unlawful love, but may she hallow peaceful married life and shrewdly decide whom each of us shall wed.

(strophe 2)

O my country, O my own dear home! God grant I may never be an outcast from my city, leading that cruel helpless life, whose every day is misery. Ere that may I this life complete and yield to death, ay, death; for there is no misery that doth surpass the loss of fatherland.

(antistrophe 2)

I have seen with mine eyes, nor from the lips of others have I the lesson learnt; no city, not one friend doth pity thee in this thine awful woe. May he perish and find no favour, whoso hath not in him honour for his friends, freely unlocking his heart to them. Never shall he be friend of mine. (MEDEA has been seated in despair on her door-step during the choral song. AEGEUS and his attendants enter.)

AEGEUS All hail, Medea! no man knoweth fairer prelude to the greeting of friends than this.

MEDEA All hail to thee likewise, Aegeus, son of wise Pandion. Whence comest thou to this land?

AEGEUS From Phoebus' ancient oracle.

MEDEA What took thee on thy travels to the prophetic centre of the earth?

AEGEUS The wish to ask how I might raise up seed unto myself.

MEDEA Pray tell me, hast thou till now dragged on a childless life?

AEGEUS I have no child owing to the visitation of some god.

MEDEA Hast thou a wife, or hast thou never known the married state?

AEGEUS I have a wife joined to me in wedlock's bond.

MEDEA What said Phoebus to thee as to children?

AEGEUS Words too subtle for man to comprehend.

MEDEA Surely I may learn the god's answer?

AEGEUS Most assuredly, for it is just thy subtle wit it needs.

MEDEA What said the god? speak, if I may hear it.

AEGEUS He bade me "not loose the wineskin's pendent neck."

MEDEA Till when? what must thou do first, what country visit?

AEGEUS Till I to my native home return.

MEDEA What object hast thou in sailing to this land?

AEGEUS O'er Troezen's realm is Pittheus king.

MEDEA Pelops' son, a man devout they say.

AEGEUS To him I fain would impart the oracle of the god.

MEDEA The man is shrewd and versed in such-like lore.

AEGEUS Aye, and to me the dearest of all my warrior friends.

MEDEA Good luck to thee! success to all thy wishes!

AEGEUS But why that downcast eye, that wasted cheek?

MEDEA O Aegeus, my husband has proved most evil.

AEGEUS What meanest thou? explain to me clearly the cause of thy despondency.

MEDEA Jason is wronging me though I have given him no cause.

AEGEUS What hath he done? tell me more clearly.

MEDEA He is taking another wife to succeed me as mistress of his house.

AEGEUS Can he have brought himself to such a dastard deed?

MEDEA Be assured thereof; I, whom he loved of yore, am in dishonour now.

AEGEUS Hath he found a new love? or does he loathe thy bed?

MEDEA Much in love is he! A traitor to his friend is he

become.

AEGEUS Enough! if he is a villain as thou sayest.

MEDEA The alliance he is so much enamoured of is with a princess.

AEGEUS Who gives his daughter to him? go on, I pray.

MEDEA Creon, who is lord of this land of Corinth.

AEGEUS Lady, I can well pardon thy grief.

MEDEA I am undone, and more than that, am banished from the land.

AEGEUS By whom? fresh woe this word of thine unfolds.

MEDEA Creon drives me forth in exile from Corinth.

AEGEUS Doth Jason allow it? This too I blame him for.

MEDEA Not in words, but he will not stand out against it. O, I implore thee by this beard and by thy knees, in suppliant posture, pity, O pity my sorrows; do not see me cast forth forlorn, but receive me in thy country, to a seat within thy halls. So may thy wish by heaven's grace be crowned with a full harvest of offspring, and may thy life close in happiness! Thou knowest not the rare good luck thou findest here, for I will make thy childlessness to cease and cause thee to beget fair issue; so potent are the spells I know.

AEGEUS Lady, on many grounds I am most fain to grant thee this thy boon, first for the gods' sake, next for the children whom thou dost promise I shall beget; for in respect of this I am completely lost. 'Tis thus with me; if e'er thou reach my land, I will attempt to champion thee as I am bound to do. Only one warning I do give thee first, lady; I will not from this land bear thee away, yet if of thyself thou reach my halls, there shalt thou bide in safety and I will never yield thee up to any man. But from this land escape without my aid, for I have no wish to incur the blame of my allies as well.

MEDEA It shall be even so; but wouldst thou pledge thy word to this, I should in all be well content with thee.

AEGEUS Surely thou dost trust me? or is there aught that troubles thee?

MEDEA Thee I trust; but Pelias' house and Creon are my foes. Wherefore, if thou art bound by an oath, thou wilt not give me up to them when they come to drag me from the land, but, having entered into a compact and sworn by heaven as well, thou wilt become my friend and disregard their overtures. Weak is any aid of mine, whilst they have wealth and a princely house.

AEGEUS Lady, thy words show much foresight, so if this is thy will, I do not, refuse. For I shall feel secure and safe if I have some pretext to offer to thy foes, and thy case too the firmer stands. Now name thy gods.

MEDEA Swear by the plain of Earth, by Helios my father's sire, and, in one comprehensive oath, by all the race of gods.

AEGEUS What shall I swear to do, from what refrain? tell me that.

MEDEA Swear that thou wilt never of thyself expel me from thy land, nor, whilst life is thine, permit any other, one of my foes maybe, to hale me thence if so he will.

AEGEUS By Earth I swear, by the Sun-god's holy beam and by all the host of heaven that I will stand fast to the terms I hear thee make.

MEDEA 'Tis enough. If thou shouldst break this oath, what curse dost thou invoke upon thyself?

AEGEUS Whate'er betides the impious.

MEDEA Go in peace; all is well, and I with what speed I may, will to thy city come, when I have wrought my purpose and obtained my wish. (AEGEUS and his retinue depart.)

CHORUS (chanting) May Maia's princely son go with

thee on thy way to bring thee to thy home, and mayest thou attain that on which thy soul is set so firmly, for to my mind thou seemest a generous man, O Aegeus.

MEDEA O Zeus, and Justice, child of Zeus, and Sun-god's light, now will triumph o'er my foes, kind friends; on victory's road have I set forth; good hope have I of wreaking vengeance on those I hate. For where we were in most distress this stranger hath appeared, to be a haven in my counsels; to him will we make fast the cables of our ship when we come to the town and citadel of Pallas. But now will I explain to thee my plans in full; do not expect to hear a pleasant tale. A servant of mine will I to Jason send and crave an interview; then when he comes I will address him with soft words, say, "this pleases me," and, "that is well," even the marriage with the princess, which my treacherous lord is celebrating, and add "it suits us both, 'twas well thought out"; then will I entreat that here my children may abide, not that I mean to leave them in a hostile land for foes to flout, but that I may slay the king's daughter by guile. For I will send them with gifts in their hands, carrying them unto the bride to save them from banishment, a robe of finest woof and a chaplet of gold. And if these ornaments she take and put them on, miserably shall she die, and likewise everyone who touches her; with such fell poisons will I smear my gifts. And here I quit this theme; but I shudder at the deed I must do next; for I will slay the children I have borne; there is none shall take them from my toils; and when I have utterly confounded Jason's house I will leave the land, escaping punishment for my dear children's murder, after my most unholy deed. For I cannot endure the taunts of enemies, kind friends; enough! what gain is life to me? I have no country, home, or refuge left. O, I did wrong, that hour I left my father's home, persuaded by that Hellene's words, who now shall pay the penalty, so help me God, Never shall he see again alive the children I bore to him, nor from his new bride shall he beget issue, for she must die a hideous death, slain by my drugs. Let no one deem me a poor weak woman who sits with folded hands, but of another mould, dangerous to foes and well-disposed to friends; for they win the fairest fame who live then, life like me.

LEADER OF THE CHORUS Since thou hast imparted this design to me, I bid thee hold thy hand, both from a wish to serve thee and because I would uphold the laws men make.

MEDEA It cannot but be so; thy words I pardon since thou art not in the same sorry plight that I am.

LEADER O lady, wilt thou steel thyself to slay thy children twain?

MEDEA I will, for that will stab my husband to the heart.

LEADER It may, but thou wilt be the saddest wife alive.

MEDEA No matter; wasted is every word that comes 'twixt now and then. Ho! (The NURSE enters in answer to her call.) Thou, go call me Jason hither, for thee I do employ on every mission of trust. No word divulge of all my purpose, as thou art to thy mistress loyal and likewise of my sex. (The NURSE goes out.)

CHORUS (singing, strophe 1)

Sons of Erechtheus, heroes happy from of yore, children of the blessed gods, fed on wisdom's glorious food in a holy land ne'er pillaged by its foes, ye who move with sprightly step through a climate ever bright and clear, where, as legend tells, the Muses nine, Pieria's holy maids, were brought to birth by Harmonia with the golden hair.

(antistrophe 1)

And poets sing how Cypris drawing water from the streams of fair-flowing Cephissus breathes o'er the land a gentle breeze of balmy winds, and ever as she crowns her tresses with a garland of sweet rose-buds sends forth the Loves to sit by wisdom's side, to take part in every excellence.

(strophe 2)

How then shall the city of sacred streams, the land that

welcomes those it loves, receive thee, the murderess of thy children, thee whose presence with others is a pollution? 'Think on the murder of thy children, consider the bloody deed thou takest on thee. Nay, by thy knees we, one and all, implore thee, slay not thy babes.

(antistrophe 2)

Where shall hand or heart find hardihood enough in wreaking such a fearsome deed upon thy sons? How wilt thou look upon thy babes, and still without a tear retain thy bloody purpose? Thou canst not, when they fall at thy feet for mercy, steel thy heart and dip in their blood thy hand. (JASON enters.)

JASON I am come at thy bidding, for e'en though thy hate for me is bitter thou shalt not fail in this small boon, but I will hear what new request thou hast to make of me, lady.

MEDEA Jason, I crave thy pardon for the words I spoke, and well thou mayest brook my burst of passion, for ere now we twain have shared much love. For I have reasoned with my soul and railed upon me thus, "Ah! poor heart! why am I thus distraught, why so angered 'gainst all good advice, why have I come to hate the rulers of the land, my husband too, who does the best for me he can, in wedding with a princess and rearing for my children noble brothers? Shall I not cease to fret? What possesses me, when heaven its best doth offer? Have I not my children to consider? do I forget that we are fugitives, in need of friends?" When I had thought all this I saw how foolish I had been, how senselessly enraged. So now do commend thee and think thee most wise in forming this connection for us; but I was mad, I who should have shared in these designs, helped on thy plans, and lent my aid to bring about the match, only too pleased to wait upon thy bride. But what we are, we are, we women, evil I will not say; wherefore thou shouldst not sink to our sorry level nor with our weapons meet our childishness.

I yield and do confess that I was wrong then, but now have I come to a better mind. Come hither, my children, come, leave the house, step forth, and with me greet and bid farewell to your father, be reconciled from all past bitterness unto your friends, as now your mother is; for we have made a truce and anger is no more. (The ATTENDANT comes out of the house with the children.) Take his right hand; ah me! my sad fate! when I reflect, as now, upon the hidden future. O my children, since there awaits you even thus a long, long life, stretch forth the hand to take a fond farewell. Ah me! how new to tears am I, how full of fear! For now that I have at last released me from my quarrel with your father, I let the tear-drops stream adown my tender cheek.

LEADER OF THE CHORUS From my eyes too bursts forth the copious tear; O, may no greater ill than the present e'er befall!

JASON Lady, I praise this conduct, not that I blame what is past; for it is but natural to the female sex to vent their spleen against a husband when he trafficks in other marriages besides his own. But thy heart is changed to wiser schemes and thou art determined on the better course, late though it be; this is acting like a woman of sober sense. And for you, my sons, hath your father provided with all good heed a sure refuge, by God's grace; for ye, I trow, shall with your brothers share hereafter the foremost rank in this Corinthian realm. Only grow up, for all the rest your sire and whoso of the gods is kind to us is bringing to pass. May I see you reach man's full estate, high o'er the heads of those I hate! But thou, lady, why with fresh tears dost thou thine eyelids wet, turning away thy wan cheek, with no welcome for these my happy tidings?

MEDEA 'Tis naught; upon these children my thoughts were turned.

JASON Then take heart; for I will see that it is well with them.

MEDEA I will do so; nor will I doubt thy word; woman is a weak creature, ever given to tears.

JASON Why prithee, unhappy one, dost moan o'er these

children?

MEDEA I gave them birth; and when thou didst pray long life for them, pity entered into my soul to think that these things must be. But the reason of thy coming hither to speak with me is partly told, the rest will I now mention. Since it is the pleasure of the rulers of the land to banish me, and well I know 'twere best for me to stand not in the way of thee or of the rulers by dwelling here, enemy as I am thought unto their house, forth from this land in exile am I going, but these children,-that they may know thy fostering hand, beg Creon to remit their banishment.

JASON I doubt whether I can persuade him, yet must I attempt it.

MEDEA At least do thou bid thy wife ask her sire this boon, to remit the exile of the children from this land.

JASON Yea, that will I; and her methinks I shall persuade, since she is woman like the rest.

MEDEA I too will aid thee in this task, for by the children's hand I will send to her gifts that far surpass in beauty, I well know, aught that now is seen 'mongst men, a robe of finest tissue and a chaplet of chased gold. But one of my attendants must haste and bring the ornaments hither. (A servant goes into the house.) Happy shall she be not once alone but ten thousand-fold, for in thee she wins the noblest soul to share her love, and gets these gifts as well which on a day my father's sire, the Sun-god, bestowed on his descendants. (The servant returns and hands the gifts to the children.) My children, take in your hands these wedding gifts, and bear them as an offering to the royal maid, the happy bride; for verily the gifts she shall receive are not to be scorned.

JASON But why so rashly rob thyself of these gifts? Dost think a royal palace wants for robes or gold? Keep them, nor give them to another. For well I know that if my lady hold me in esteem, she will set my price above all wealth.

MEDEA Say not so; 'tis said that gifts tempt even gods;

and o'er men's minds gold holds more potent sway than count-less words. Fortune smiles upon thy bride, and heaven now doth swell her triumph; youth is hers and princely power; yet to save my children from exile I would barter life, not dross alone. Children, when we are come to the rich palace, pray your father's new bride, my mistress, with suppliant voice to save you from exile, offering her these ornaments the while; for it is most needful that she receive the gifts in her own hand. Now go and linger not; may ye succeed and to your mother bring back the glad tidings she fain would hear (JASON, the ATTENDANT, and the children go out together.)

CHORUS (singing, strophe 1)

Gone, gone is every hope I had that the children yet might live; forth to their doom they now proceed. The hapless bride will take, ay, take the golden crown that is to be her ruin; with her own hand will she lift and place upon her golden locks the garniture of death.

(antistrophe 1)

Its grace and sheen divine will tempt her to put on the robe and crown of gold, and in that act will she deck herself to be a bride amid the dead. Such is the snare whereinto she will fall, such is the deadly doom that waits the hapless maid, nor shall she from the curse escape.

(strophe 2)

And thou, poor wretch, who to thy sorrow art wedding a king's daughter, little thinkest of the doom thou art bringing on thy children's life, or of the cruel death that waits thy bride. Woe is thee! how art thou fallen from thy high estate!

(antistrophe 2)

Next do I bewail thy sorrows, O mother hapless in thy children, thou who wilt slay thy babes because thou hast a rival, the babes thy husband hath deserted impiously to join him to another bride. (The ATTENDANT enters with the children.)

ATTENDANT Thy children, lady, are from exile freed, and gladly did the royal bride accept thy gifts in her own hands, and so thy children made their peace with her.

MEDEA Ah!

ATTENDANT Why art so disquieted in thy prosperous hour? Why turnest thou thy cheek away, and hast no welcome for my glad news?

MEDEA Ah me!

ATTENDANT These groans but ill accord with the news I bring.

MEDEA Ah me! once more I say.

ATTENDANT Have I unwittingly announced some evil tidings? Have I erred in thinking my news was good?

MEDEA Thy news is as it is; I blame thee not.

ATTENDANT Then why this downcast eye, these floods of tears?

MEDEA Old friend, needs must I weep; for the gods and I with fell intent devised these schemes.

ATTENDANT Be of good cheer; thou too of a surety shalt by thy sons yet be brought home again.

MEDEA Ere that shall I bring others to their home, ah! woe is me

ATTENDANT Thou art not the only mother from thy children reft. Bear patiently thy troubles as a mortal must.

MEDEA I will obey; go thou within the house and make the day's provision for the children. (The ATTENDANT enters the house. MEDEA turns to the children.) O my babes, my babes, ye have still a city and a home, where far from me and my sad lot you will live your lives, reft of your mother for ever; while I must to another land in banishment, or ever I have had my joy of you, or lived to see you happy, or ever I have graced your marriage couch, your bride, your bridal

bower, or lifted high the wedding torch. Ah me! a victim of
my own self-will. So it was all in vain I reared you, O my
sons; in vain did suffer, racked with anguish, enduring the
cruel pangs of childbirth. 'Fore Heaven I once had hope, poor
me! high hope of ye that you would nurse me in my age and
deck my corpse with loving hands, a boon we mortals covet;
but now is my sweet fancy dead and gone; for I must lose you
both and in bitterness and sorrow drag through life. And ye
shall never with fond eyes see your mother more for o'er your
life there comes a change. Ah me! ah me! why do ye look at
me so, my children? why smile that last sweet smile? Ah me!
what am I to do? My heart gives way when I behold my children's laughing eyes. O, I cannot; farewell to all my former
schemes; I will take the children from the land, the babes I
bore. Why should I wound their sire by wounding them, and
get me a twofold measure of sorrow? No, no, I will not do it.
Farewell my scheming! And yet what possesses me? Can I
consent to let those foes of mine escape from punishment,
and incur their mockery? I must face this deed. Out upon
my craven heart! to think that I should even have let the
soft words escape my soul. Into the house, children! (The
children go into the house.) And whoso feels he must not
be present at my sacrifice, must see to it himself; I will not
spoil my handiwork. Ah! ah! do not, my heart, O do not do
this deed! Let the children go, unhappy one, spare the babes!
For if they live, they will cheer thee in our exile there. Nay,
by the fiends of hell's abyss, never, never will I hand my children over to their foes to mock and flout. Die they must in
any case, and since 'tis so, why I, the mother who bore them,
will give the fatal blow. In any case their doom is fixed and
there is no escape. Already the crown is on her head, the robe
is round her, and she is dying, the royal bride; that do I know
full well. But now since I have a piteous path to tread, and
yet more piteous still the path I send my children on, fain
would I say farewell to them. (The children come out at her
call. She takes them in her arms.) O my babes, my babes, let
your mother kiss your hands. Ah! hands I love so well, O lips
most dear to me! O noble form and features of my children, I
wish ye joy, but in that other land, for here your father robs

you of your home. O the sweet embrace, the soft young cheek, the fragrant breath! my children! Go, leave me; I cannot bear to longer look upon ye; my sorrow wins the day. At last I understand the awful deed I am to do; but passion, that cause of direst woes to mortal man, hath triumphed o'er my sober thoughts. (She goes into the house with the children.)

CHORUS (chanting) Oft ere now have I pursued subtler themes and have faced graver issues than woman's sex should seek to probe; but then e'en we aspire to culture, which dwells with us to teach us wisdom; I say not all; for small is the class amongst women-(one maybe shalt thou find 'mid many)-that is not incapable of wisdom. And amongst mortals I do assert that they who are wholly without experience and have never had children far surpass in happiness those who are parents. The childless, because they have never proved whether children grow up to be a blessing or curse to men are removed from all share in many troubles; whilst those who have a sweet race of children growing up in their houses do wear away, as I perceive, their whole life through; first with the thought how they may train them up in virtue, next how they shall leave their sons the means to live; and after all this 'tis far from clear whether on good or bad children they bestow their toil. But one last crowning woe for every mortal man now will name; suppose that they have found sufficient means to live, and seen their children grow to man's estate and walk in virtue's path, still if fortune so befall, comes Death and bears the children's bodies off to Hades. Can it be any profit to the gods to heap upon us mortal men beside our other woes this further grief for children lost, a grief surpassing all? (MEDEA comes out of the house.)

MEDEA Kind friends, long have I waited expectantly to know how things would at the palace chance. And lo! I see one of Jason's servants coming hither, whose hurried gasps for breath proclaim him the bearer of some fresh tidings. (A MESSENGER rushes in.)

MESSENGER Fly, fly, Medea! who hast wrought an awful deed, transgressing every law: nor leave behind or seaborne bark or car that scours the plain.

MEDEA Why, what hath chanced that calls for such a flight of mine?

MESSENGER The princess is dead, a moment gone, and Creon too, her sire, slain by those drugs of thine.

MEDEA Tidings most fair are thine! Henceforth shalt thou be ranked amongst my friends and benefactors.

MESSENGER Ha! What? Art sane? Art not distraught, lady, who hearest with joy the outrage to our royal house done, and art not at the horrid tale afraid?

MEDEA Somewhat have I, too, to say in answer to thy words. Be not so hasty, friend, but tell the manner of their death, for thou wouldst give me double joy, if so they perished miserably.

MESSENGER When the children twain whom thou didst bear came with their father and entered the palace of the bride, right glad were we thralls who had shared thy griefs, for instantly from ear to ear a rumour spread that thou and thy lord had made up your former quarrel. One kissed thy children's hands, another their golden hair, while I for very joy went with them in person to the women's chambers. Our mistress, whom now we do revere in thy room, cast a longing glance at Jason, ere she saw thy children twain; but then she veiled her eyes and turned her blanching cheek away, disgusted at their coming; but thy husband tried to check his young bride's angry humour with these words: "O, be not angered 'gainst thy friends; cease from wrath and turn once more thy face this way, counting as friends whomso thy husband counts, and accept these gifts, and for my sake crave thy sire to remit these children's exile." Soon as she saw the ornaments, no longer she held out, but yielded to her lord in all; and ere the father and his sons were far from the palace gone, she took the broidered robe and put it on, and set the golden crown about her tresses, arranging her hair at her bright mirror, with many a happy smile at her breathless counterfeit. Then rising from her seat she passed across the chamber, tripping lightly on her fair white foot, exulting in the gift, with many a glance at her uplifted ankle. When lo! a scene of awful horror did ensue. In a moment she turned pale, reeled backwards, trembling in every limb, and sinks upon a seat scarce soon enough to save herself from falling to the ground. An aged dame, one of her company, thinking belike it was a fit from Pan or some god sent, raised a cry of prayer, till from her mouth she saw the foam-flakes issue, her eyeballs rolling in their sockets, and all the blood her face desert; then did she raise a loud scream far different from her former cry. Forthwith one handmaid rushed to her father's house, another to her new bridegroom to tell his bride's sad fate, and the whole house echoed with their running to and fro. By this time would a quick walker have made the turn in a course of six plethra and reached the goal, when she with one awful shriek awoke, poor sufferer, from her speechless trance and oped her closed eyes, for against her a twofold anguish was warring. The chaplet of gold about her head was sending forth a wondrous stream of ravening flame, while the fine raiment, thy children's gift, was preying on the hapless maiden's fair white flesh; and she starts from her seat in a blaze and seeks to fly, shaking her hair and head this way and that, to cast the crown therefrom; but the gold held firm to its fastenings, and the flame, as she shook her locks, blazed forth the more with double fury. Then to the earth she sinks, by the cruel blow o'ercome; past all recognition now save to a father's eye; for her eyes had lost their tranquil gaze, her face no more its natural look preserved, and from the crown of her head blood and fire in mingled stream ran down; and from her bones the flesh kept peeling off beneath the gnawing of those secret drugs, e'en as when the pine-tree weeps its tears of pitch, a fearsome sight to see. And all were afraid to touch the corpse, for we were warned by what had chanced. Anon came her haples father unto the house, all unwitting of her doom, and stumbles o'er the dead, and loud he cried, and folding his arms about her kissed her, with words like these the while, "O my poor, poor child, which of the gods hath destroyed thee thus foully? Who is robbing me of thee, old as I am and ripe for death? O my child, alas! would I could die with thee!" He ceased his sad lament, and would have raised his aged frame, but found himself held fast by the fine-spun robe as ivy that clings to the branches of the bay, and then ensued a fearful struggle. He strove to rise, but she still held him back; and if ever he pulled with all his might, from off his bones his aged flesh he tore. At last he gave it up, and breathed forth his soul in awful suffering; for he could no longer master the pain. So there they lie, daughter and aged sire, dead side by side, a grievous sight that calls for tears. And as for thee, I leave thee out of my consideration, for thyself must discover a means to escape punishment. Not now for the first time I think this human life a shadow; yea, and without shrinking I will say that they amongst men who pretend to wisdom and expend deep thought on words do incur a serious charge of folly; for amongst mortals no man is happy; wealth may pour in and make one luckier than another, but none can happy be. (The MESSENGER departs.)

LEADER OF THE CHORUS This day the deity, it seems, will mass on Jason, as he well deserves, heavy load of evils. Woe is thee, daughter of Creon We pity thy sad fate, gone as thou art to Hades' halls as the price of thy marriage with Jason.

MEDEA My friends, I am resolved upon the deed; at once will I slay my children and then leave this land, without delaying long enough to hand them over to some more savage hand to butcher. Needs must they die in any case; and since they must, I will slay them-I, the mother that bare them. O heart of mine, steel thyself! Why do I hesitate to do the awful deed that must be done? Come, take the sword, thou wretched hand of mine! Take it, and advance to the post whence starts thy life of sorrow! Away with cowardice! Give not one thought to thy babes, how dear they are or how thou art their mother. This one brief day forget thy children dear, and after that lament; for though thou wilt slay them yet they were thy darlings still, and I am a lady of sorrows. (MEDEA enters the house.)

CHORUS (chanting) O earth, O sun whose beam illumines all, look, look upon this lost woman, ere she stretch forth her murderous hand upon her sons for blood; for lo! these are scions of thy own golden seed, and the blood of gods is in danger of being shed by man. O light, from Zeus proceeding, stay her, hold her hand, forth from the house chase this fell bloody fiend by demons led. Vainly wasted were the throes thy children cost thee; vainly hast thou borne, it seems, sweet babes, O thou who hast left behind thee that passage through the blue Symplegades, that strangers justly hate. Ah! hapless one, why doth fierce anger thy soul assail? Why in its place is fell murder growing up? For grievous unto mortal men are pollutions that come of kindred blood poured on the earth, woes to suit each crime hurled from heaven on the murderer's house.

FIRST SON (within) Ah, me; what can I do? Whither fly to escape my mother's blows?

SECOND SON (within) I know not, sweet brother mine; we are lost.

CHORUS (chanting) Didst hear, didst hear the children's cry? O lady, born to sorrow, victim of an evil fate! Shall I enter the house? For the children's sake I am resolved to ward off the murder.

FIRST SON (within) Yea, by heaven I adjure you; help, your aid is needed.

SECOND SON (within) Even now the toils of the sword are closing round us.

CHORUS (chanting) O hapless mother, surely thou hast a heart of stone or steel to slay the offspring of thy womb by such a murderous doom. Of all the wives of yore I know but one who laid her hand upon her children dear, even Ino, whom the gods did madden in the day that the wife of Zeus drove her wandering from her home. But she, poor sufferer, flung herself into the sea because of the foul murder of her children, leaping o'er the wave-beat cliff, and in her death was she united to her children twain. Can there be any deed of horror left to follow this? Woe for the wooing of women fraught with disaster! What sorrows hast thou caused for men ere now! (JASON and his attendants enter.)

JASON Ladies, stationed near this house, pray tell me is the author of these hideous deeds, Medea, still within, or hath she fled from hence? For she must hide beneath the earth or soar on wings towards heaven's vault, if she would avoid the vengeance of the royal house. Is she so sure she will escape herself unpunished from this house, when she hath slain the rulers of the land? But enough of this! I am forgetting her children. As for her, those whom she hath wronged will do the like by her; but I am come to save the children's life, lest the victim's kin visit their wrath on me, in vengeance for the murder foul, wrought by my children's mother.

LEADER OF THE CHORUS Unhappy man, thou knowest not the full extent of thy misery, else had thou never said those words.

JASON How now? Can she want to kill me too?

LEADER Thy sons are dead; slain by their own mother's hand.

JASON O God! what sayest thou? Woman, thou hast sealed my doom.

LEADER Thy children are no more; be sure of this.

JASON Where slew she them; within the palace or outside?

LEADER Throw wide the doors and see thy children's murdered corpses.

JASON Haste, ye slaves, loose the bolts, undo the fastenings, that I may see the sight of twofold woe, my murdered sons and her, whose blood in vengeance I will shed. (MEDEA appears above the house, on a chariot drawn by dragons; the children's corpses are beside her.)

MEDEA Why shake those doors and attempt to loose their bolts, in quest of the dead and me their murderess? From such toil desist. If thou wouldst aught with me, say on, if so thou wilt; but never shalt thou lay hand on me, so swift the steeds the sun, my father's sire, to me doth give to save me from the hand of my foes.

JASON Accursed woman! by gods, by me and all mankind abhorred as never woman was, who hadst the heart to stab thy babes, thou their mother, leaving me undone and childless; this hast thou done and still dost gaze upon the sun and earth after this deed most impious. Curses on thee! now perceive what then I missed in the day I brought thee, fraught with doom, from thy home in a barbarian land to dwell in Hellas, traitress to thy sire and to the land that nurtured thee. On me the gods have hurled the curse that dogged thy steps, for thou didst slay thy brother at his hearth ere thou cam'st aboard our fair ship, Argo. Such was the outset of thy life of crime; then didst thou wed with me, and having borne me sons to glut thy passion's lust, thou now hast slain them. Not one amongst the wives of Hellas e'er had dared this deed; yet before them all I chose thee for my wife, wedding a foe to be my doom, no woman, but a lioness fiercer than Tyrrhene Scylla in nature. But with reproaches heaped thousandfold I cannot wound thee, so brazen is thy nature. Perish, vile sorceress, murderess of thy babes! Whilst I must mourn my luckless fate, for I shall ne'er enjoy my new-found bride, nor shall I have the children, whom I bred and reared, alive to say the last farewell to me; nay, I have lost them.

MEDEA To this thy speech I could have made a long reply, but Father Zeus knows well all I have done for thee, and the treatment thou hast given me. Yet thou wert not ordained to scorn my love and lead a life of joy in mockery of me, nor was thy royal bride nor Creon, who gave thee a second wife, to thrust me from this land and rue it not. Wherefore, if thou wilt, call me e'en a lioness, and Scylla, whose home is in the Tyrrhene land; for I in turn have wrung thy heart, as well I might.

JASON Thou, too, art grieved thyself, and sharest in my sorrow.

MEDEA Be well assured I am; but it relieves my pain to

know thou canst not mock at me.

JASON O my children, how vile a mother ye have found!

MEDEA My sons, your father's feeble lust has been your ruin!

JASON 'Twas not my hand, at any rate, that slew them.

MEDEA No, but thy foul treatment of me, and thy new marriage.

JASON Didst think that marriage cause enough to murder them?

MEDEA Dost think a woman counts this a trifling injury?

JASON So she be self-restrained; but in thy eyes all is evil.

MEDEA Thy sons are dead and gone. That will stab thy heart.

JASON They live, methinks, to bring a curse upon thy head.

MEDEA The gods know, whoso of them began this troublous coil.

JASON Indeed, they know that hateful heart of thine.

MEDEA Thou art as hateful. I am aweary of thy bitter tongue.

JASON And I likewise of thine. But parting is easy.

MEDEA Say how; what am I to do? for I am fain as thou to go.

JASON Give up to me those dead, to bury and lament.

MEDEA No, never! I will bury them myself, bearing them to Hera's sacred field, who watches o'er the Cape, that none of their foes may insult them by pulling down their tombs; and in this land of Sisyphus I will ordain hereafter a solemn feast and mystic rites to atone for this impious murder. Myself will now to the land of Erechtheus, to dwell with Aegeus, Pandion's son. But thou, as well thou mayst, shalt die a caitiff's death, thy head crushed 'neath a shattered relic of Argo, when thou hast seen the bitter ending of my marriage.

JASON The curse of our sons' avenging spirit and of justice, that calls for blood, be on thee!

MEDEA What god or power divine hears thee, breaker of oaths and every law of hospitality?

JASON Fie upon thee! cursed witch! child-murderess!

MEDEA To thy house! go, bury thy wife.

JASON I go, bereft of both my sons.

MEDEA Thy grief is yet to come; wait till old age is with thee too.

JASON O my dear, dear children!

MEDEA Dear to their mother, not to thee.

JASON And yet thou didst slay them?

MEDEA Yea, to vex thy heart.

JASON One last fond kiss, ah me! I fain would on their lips imprint.

MEDEA Embraces now, and fond farewells for them; but then a cold repulse!

JASON By heaven I do adjure thee, let me touch their tender skin.

MEDEA No, no! in vain this word has sped its flight.

JASON O Zeus, dost hear how I am driven hence; dost mark the treatment I receive from this she-lion, fell murderess of her young? Yet so far as I may and can, I raise for them a dirge, and do adjure the gods to witness how thou hast slain my sons, and wilt not suffer me to embrace or bury their dead bodies. Would I had never begotten them to see thee slay them after all! (The chariot carries MEDEA away.)

CHORUS (chanting) Many a fate doth Zeus dispense, high on his Olympian throne; oft do the gods bring things to pass beyond man's expectation; that, which we thought would be, is not fulfilled, while for the unlooked-for god finds out a way; and such hath been the issue of this matter.

THE END

The Bachae

Dramatis Personae

Dionysus
Cadmus
Pentheus
Agave
Teiresias
First Messenger
Second Messenger
Servant

Before the Palace of Pentheus at Thebes. Enter DIONY-
SUS.

DIONYSUS Lo! I am come to this land of Thebes, Dionysus' the son of Zeus, of whom on a day Semele, the daughter
of Cadmus, was delivered by a flash of lightning. I have put
off the god and taken human shape, and so present myself at
Dirce's springs and the waters of Ismenus. Yonder I see my
mother's monument where the bolt slew her nigh her house,
and there are the ruins of her home smouldering with the
heavenly flame that blazeth still-Hera's deathless outrage on
my mother. To Cadmus all praise I offer, because he keeps
this spot hallowed, his daughter's precinct, which my own
hands have shaded round about with the vine's clustering
foliage.

Lydia's glebes, where gold abounds, and Phrygia have I

left behind; o'er Persia's sun-baked plains, by Bactria's walled towns and Media's wintry clime have I advanced through Arabia, land of promise; and Asia's length and breadth, outstretched along the brackish sea, with many a fair walled town, peopled with mingled race of Hellenes and barbarians; and this is the first city in Hellas I have reached. There too have I ordained dances and established my rites, that I might manifest my godhead to men; but Thebes is the first city in the land of Hellas that I have made ring with shouts of joy, girt in a fawn-skin, with a thyrsus, my ivy-bound spear, in my hand; since my mother's sisters, who least of all should have done it, denied that Dionysus was the son of Zeus, saying that Semele, when she became a mother by some mortal lover, tried to foist her sin on Zeus-a clever ruse of Cadmus, which, they boldly asserted, caused Zeus to slay her for the falsehood about the marriage. Wherefore these are they whom I have driven frenzied from their homes, and they are dwelling on the hills with mind distraught; and I have forced them to assume the dress worn in my orgies, and all the women-folk of Cadmus' stock have I driven raving from their homes, one and all alike; and there they sit upon the roofless rocks beneath the green pine-trees, mingling amongst the sons of Thebes. For this city must learn, however loth, seeing that it is not initiated in my Bacchic rites, and I must take up my mother's defence, by showing to mortals that the child she bore to Zeus is a deity. Now Cadmus gave his sceptre and its privileges to Pentheus, his daughter's child, who wages war 'gainst my divinity, thrusting me away from his drink-offerings, and making no mention of me in his prayers. Therefore will I prove to him and all the race of Cadmus that I am a god. And when I have set all in order here, I will pass hence to a fresh country, manifesting myself; but if the city of Thebes in fury takes up arms and seeks to drive my votaries from the mountain, I will meet them at the head of my frantic rout. This is why I have assumed a mortal form, and put off my godhead to take man's nature.

O ye who left Tmolus, the bulwark of Lydia, ye women, my revel rout! whom I brought from your foreign homes to be ever by my side and bear me company, uplift the cymbals

native to your Phrygian home, that were by me and the great
mother Rhea first devised, and march around the royal halls
of Pentheus smiting them, that the city of Cadmus may see
you; while I will seek Cithaeron's glens, there with my Bacchanals to join the dance. (Exit DIONYSUS., Enter CHO-
RUS.)

CHORUS From Asia o'er the holy ridge of Tmolus hasten to a pleasant task, a toil that brings no weariness, for
Bromius' sake, in honour of the Bacchic god. Who loiters in
the road? who lingers 'neath the roof? Avaunt! I say, and
let every lip be hushed in solemn silence; for I will raise a
hymn to Dionysus, as custom aye ordains. O happy he! who
to his joy is initiated in heavenly mysteries and leads a
holy life, joining heart and soul in Bacchic revelry upon the
hills, purified from every sin; observing the rites of Cybele,
the mighty mother, and brandishing the thyrsus, with ivy-
wreathed head, he worships Dionysus. Go forth, go forth, ye
Bacchanals, bring home the Bromian god Dionysus, child of
a god, from the mountains of Phrygia to the spacious streets
of Hellas, bring home the Bromian god! whom on a day his
mother in her sore travail brought forth untimely, yielding
up her life beneath the lightning stroke of Zeus' winged bolt;
but forthwith Zeus, the son of Cronos, found for him another
womb wherein to rest, for he hid him in his thigh and fas-
tened it with golden pins to conceal him from Hera. And when
the Fates had fully formed the horned god, he brought him
forth and crowned him with a coronal of snakes, whence it is
the thyrsus-bearing Maenads hunt the snake to twine about
their hair. O Thebes, nurse of Semele! crown thyself with ivy;
burst forth, burst forth with blossoms fair of green convolvulus, and with the boughs of oak and pine join in the Bacchic
revelry; dor;-thy coat of dappled fawn-skin, decking it with
tufts of silvered hair; with reverent hand the sportive wand
now wield. Anon shall the whole land be dancing, when Bromius leads his revellers to the hills, to the hills away! where
wait him groups of maidens from loom and shuttle roused in
frantic haste by Dionysus. O hidden cave of the Curetes! O
hallowed haunts in Crete, that saw Zeus born, where Cory-
bantes with crested helms devised for me in their grotto the

rounded timbrel of ox-hide, mingling Bacchic minstrelsy with the shrill sweet accents of the Phrygian flute, a gift bestowed by them on mother Rhea, to add its crash of music to the Bacchantes' shouts of joy; but frantic satyrs won it from the mother-goddess for their own, and added it to their dances in festivals, which gladden the heart of Dionysus, each third recurrent year. Oh! happy that votary, when from the hurrying revel-rout he sinks to earth, in his holy robe of fawnskin, chasing the goat to drink its blood, a banquet sweet of flesh uncooked, as he hastes to Phrygia's or to Libya's hills; while in the van the Bromian god exults with cries of Evoe. With milk and wine and streams of luscious honey flows the earth, and Syrian incense smokes. While the Bacchante holding in his hand a blazing torch of pine uplifted on his wand waves it, as he speeds along, rousing wandering votaries, and as he waves it cries aloud with wanton tresses tossing in the breeze; and thus to crown the revelry, he raises loud his voice, "On, on, ye Bacchanals, pride of Tmolus with its rills of gold I to the sound of the booming drum, chanting in joyous strains the praises of your joyous god with Phrygian accents lifted high, what time the holy lute with sweet complaining note invites you to your hallowed sport, according well with feet that hurry wildly to the hills; like a colt that gambols at its mother's side in the pasture, with gladsome heart each Bacchante bounds along." (Enter TEIRESIAS.)

TEIRESIAS What loiterer at the gates will call Cadmus from the house, Agenor's son, who left the city of Sidon and founded here the town of Thebes? Go one of you, announce to him that Teiresias is seeking him; he knows himself the reason of my coming and the compact I and he have made in our old age to bind the thyrsus with leaves and don the fawnskin, crowning our heads the while with ivy-sprays. (Enter CADMUS.)

CADMUS Best of friends! I was in the house when I heard thy voice, wise as its owner. I come prepared, dressed in the livery of the god. For 'tis but right I should magnify with all my might my own daughter's son, Dionysus, who hath shown his godhead unto men. Where are we to join the dance? where plant the foot and shake the hoary head? Do thou, Teiresias, be my guide, age leading age, for thou art wise. Never shall I weary, night or day, of beating the earth with my thyrsus. What joy to forget our years?

TEIRESIAS Why, then thou art as I am. For I too am young again, and will essay the dance.

CADMUS We will drive then in our chariot to the hill.

TEIRESIAS Nay, thus would the god not have an equal honour paid.

CADMUS Well, I will lead thee, age leading age.

TEIRESIAS The god will guide us both thither without toil.

CADMUS Shall we alone of all the city dance in Bacchus' honour?

TEIRESIAS Yea, for we alone are wise, the rest are mad.

CADMUS We stay too long; come, take my hand.

TEIRESIAS There link thy hand in my firm grip.

CADMUS Mortal that I am, I scorn not the gods.

TEIRESIAS No subtleties do I indulge about the powers of heaven. The faith we inherited from our fathers, old as time itself, no reasoning shall cast down; no! though it were the subtlest invention of wits refined. Maybe some one will say, I have no respect for my grey hair in going to dance with ivy round my head; not so, for the god did not define whether old or young should dance, but from all alike he claims a universal homage, and scorns nice calculations in his worship.

CADMUS Teiresias, since thou art blind, I must prompt thee what to say. Pentheus is coming hither to the house in haste, Echion's son, to whom I resign the government. How scared he looks I what strange tidings will he tell? (Enter PENTHEUS.)

PENTHEUS I had left my kingdom for awhile, when tidings of strange mischief in this city reached me; I hear that our women-folk have left their homes on pretence of Bacchic rites, and on the wooded hills rush wildly to and fro, honouring in the dance this new god Dionysus, whoe'er he is; and in the midst of each revel-rout the brimming wine-bowl stands, and one by one they steal away to lonely spots to gratify their lust, pretending forsooth that they are Maenads bent on sacrifice, though it is Aphrodite they are placing before the Bacchic god. As many as I caught, my gaolers are keeping safe in the public prison fast bound; and all who are gone forth, will I chase from the hills, Ino and Agave too who bore me to Echion, and Actaeon's mother Autonoe. In fetters of iron will I bind them and soon put an end to these outrageous Bacchic rites. They say there came a stranger hither, a trickster and a sorcerer, from Lydia's land, with golden hair and perfumed locks, the flush of wine upon his face, and in his eyes each grace that Aphrodite gives; by day and night he lingers in our maidens' company on the plea of teaching Bacchic mysteries. Once let me catch him within these walls, and I will put an end to his thyrsus-beating and his waving of his tresses, for I will cut his head from his body. This is the fellow who says that Dionysus is a god, says that he was once stitched up in the thigh of Zeus-that child who with his mother was blasted by the lightning flash, because the woman falsely said her marriage was with Zeus. Is not this enough to deserve the awful penalty of hanging, this stranger's wanton insolence, whoe'er he be?

But lo! another marvel. I see Teiresias, our diviner, dressed in dappled fawn-skins, and my mother's father too, wildly waving the Bacchic wand; droll sight enough! Father, it grieves me to see you two old men so void of sense. Oh! shake that ivy from thee! Let fall the thyrsus from thy hand, my mother's sire! Was it thou, Teiresias, urged him on to this? Art bent on introducing this fellow as another new deity amongst men, that thou mayst then observe the fowls of the air and make a gain from fiery divination? Were it not that thy grey hairs protected thee, thou shouldst sit in chains amid the Bacchanals, for introducing knavish mysteries; for where the gladsome grape is found at women's feasts, I deny that their rites have any longer good results.

CHORUS What impiety! Hast thou no reverence, sir stranger, for the gods or for Cadmus who sowed the crop of earth-born warriors? Son of Echion as thou art, thou dost shame thy birth.

TEIRESIAS Whenso a man of wisdom finds a good topic for argument, it is no difficult matter to speak well; but thou, though possessing a glib tongue as if endowed with sense, art yet devoid thereof in all thou sayest. A headstrong man, if he have influence and a capacity for speaking, makes a bad citizen because he lacks sense. This new deity, whom thou deridest, will rise to power I cannot say how great, throughout Hellas. Two things there are, young prince, that hold first rank among men, the goddess Demeter, that is, the earth, calf her which name thou please; she it is that feedeth men with solid food; and as her counterpart came this god, the son of Semele, who discovered the juice of the grape and introduced it to mankind, stilling thereby each grief that mortals suffer from, soon as e'er they are filled with the juice of the vine; and sleep also he giveth, sleep that brings forgetfulness of daily ills, the sovereign charm for all our woe. God though he is, he serves all other gods for libations, so that through him mankind is blest. He it is whom thou dost mock, because he was sewn up in the thigh of Zeus. But I will show thee this fair mystery. When Zeus had snatched him from the lightning's blaze, and to Olympus borne the tender babe, Hera would have cast him forth from heaven, but Zeus, as such a god well might, devised a counterplot. He broke off a fragment of the ether which surrounds the world, and made thereof a hostage against Hera's bitterness, while he gave out Dionysus into other hands; hence, in time, men said that he was reared in the thigh of Zeus, having changed the word and invented a legend, because the god was once a hostage to the goddess Hera. This god too hath prophetic power, for there is no small prophecy inspired by Bacchic frenzy; for whenever the god in his full might enters the human frame, he makes his frantic votaries foretell the future. Likewise he hath some share in Ares' rights; for oft, or ever a weapon is touched, a panic seizes an army when it is marshalled in array; and this too is a frenzy sent by Dionysus. Yet shalt thou behold him e'en on Delphi's rocks leaping o'er the cloven height, torch in hand, waving and brandishing the branch by Bacchus loved, yea, and through the length and breadth of Hellas. Hearken to me, Pentheus; never boast that might alone doth sway the world, nor if thou think so, unsound as thy opinion is, credit thyself with any wisdom; but receive the god into thy realm, pour out libations, join the revel rout, and crown thy head. It is not Dionysus that will force chastity on women in their love; but this is what we should consider, whether chastity is part of their nature for good and all; for if it is, no really modest maid will ever fall 'mid Bacchic mysteries. Mark this: thou thyself art glad when thousands throng thy gates, and citizens extol the name of Pentheus; he too, I trow, delights in being honoured. Wherefore I and Cadmus, whom thou jeerest so, will wreath our brows with ivy and join the dance; pair of grey beards though we be, still must we take part therein; never will I for any words of thine fight against heaven. Most grievous is thy madness, nor canst thou find a charm to cure thee, albeit charms have caused thy malady.

CHORUS Old sir, thy words do not discredit Phoebus, and thou art wise in honouring Bromius, potent deity.

CADMUS My son, Teiresias hath given thee sound advice; dwell with us, but o'erstep not the threshold of custom; for now thou art soaring aloft, and thy wisdom is no wisdom. E'en though he be no god, as thou assertest, still say he is; be guilty of a splendid fraud, declaring him the son of Semele, that she may be thought the mother of a god, and we and all our race gain honour. Dost thou mark the awful fate of Actaeon? whom savage hounds of his own rearing rent in pieces in the meadows, because he boasted himself a better hunter than Artemis. Lest thy fate be the same, come let me crown thy head with ivy; join us in rendering homage to the god.

PENTHEUS Touch me not away to thy Bacchic rites thyself! never try to infect me with thy foolery! Vengeance will

I have on the fellow who teaches thee such senselessness. Away one of you without delay! seek yonder seat where he observes his birds, wrench it from its base with levers, turn it upside down, o'erthrowing it in utter confusion, and toss his garlands to the tempest's blast. For by so doing shall I wound him most deeply. Others of you range the city and hunt down this girl-faced stranger, who is introducing a new complaint amongst our women, and doing outrage to the marriage tie. And if haply ye catch him, bring him hither to me in chains, to be stoned to death, a bitter ending to his revelry in Thebes. (Exit PENTHEUS.)

TEIRESIAS Unhappy wretch! thou little knowest what thou art saying. Now art thou become a raving madman, even before unsound in mind. Let us away, Cadmus, and pray earnestly for him, spite of his savage temper, and likewise for the city, that the god inflict not a signal vengeance. Come, follow me with thy ivy-wreathed staff; try to support my tottering frame as I do thine, for it is unseemly that two old men should fall; but let that-pass. For we must serve the Bacchic god, the son of Zeus. Only, Cadmus, beware lest Pentheus' bring sorrow to thy house; it is not my prophetic art, but circumstances that lead me to say this; for the words of a fool are folly. (Exeunt CADMUS and TEIRESIAS.)

CHORUS O holiness, queen amongst the gods, sweeping on golden pinion o'er the earth! dost hear the words of Pentheus, dost hear his proud blaspheming Bromius, the son of Semele; first of all the blessed gods at every merry festival? His it is to rouse the revellers to dance, to laugh away dull care, and wake the flute, whene'er at banquets of the gods the luscious grape appears, or when the winecup in the feast sheds sleep on men who wear the ivy-spray. The end of all unbridled speech and lawless senselessness is misery; but the life of calm repose and the rule of reason abide unshaken and support the home; for far away in heaven though they dwell, the powers divine behold man's state. Sophistry is not wisdom, and to indulge in thoughts beyond man's ken is to shorten life; and if a man on such poor terms should aim too high, he may miss the pleasures in his reach. These, to my mind, are the ways of madmen and idiots. Oh! to make my way to Cyprus, isle of Aphrodite, where dwell the love-gods strong to soothe man's soul, or to Paphos, which that foreign river, never fed by rain, enriches with its hundred mouths! Oh! lead me, Bromian god, celestial guide of Bacchic pilgrims, to the hallowed slopes of Olympus, where Pierian Muses have their haunt most fair. There dwell the Graces; there is soft desire; there thy votaries may hold their revels freely. The joy of our god, the son of Zeus, is in banquets, his delight is in peace, that giver of riches and nurse divine of youth. Both to rich and poor alike hath he granted the delight of wine, that makes all pain to cease; hateful to him is every one who careth not to live the life of bliss, that lasts through days and nights of joy. True wisdom is to keep the heart and soul aloof from over-subtle wits. That which the less enlightened crowd approves and practises, will I accept. (Re-enter PENTHEUS. Enter SERVANT bringing DIONY-SUS bound.)

SERVANT We are come, Pentheus, having hunted down this prey, for which thou didst send us forth; not in vain hath been our quest. We found our quarry tame; he did not fly from us, but yielded himself without a struggle; his cheek ne'er blanched, nor did his ruddy colour change, but with a smile he bade me bind and lead him away, and he waited, making my task an easy one. For very shame I said to him, "Against my will, sir stranger, do I lead thee hence, but Pentheus ordered it, who sent me hither." As for his votaries whom thou thyself didst check, seizing and binding them hand and foot in the public gaol, all these have loosed their bonds and fled into the meadows where they now are sporting, calling aloud on the Bromian god. Their chains fell off their feet of their own accord, and doors flew open without man's hand to help. Many a marvel hath this stranger brought with him to our city of Thebes; what yet remains must be thy care.

PENTHEUS Loose his hands; for now that I have him in the net he is scarce swift enough to elude me. So, sir stranger, thou art not ill-favoured from a woman's point of view, which was thy real object in coming to Thebes; thy hair is long because thou hast never been a wrestler, flowing right down thy cheeks most wantonly; thy skin is white to help thee gain thy end, not tanned by ray of sun, but kept within the shade, as thou goest in quest of love with beauty's bait. Come, tell me first of thy race.

DIONYSUS That needs no braggart's tongue, 'tis easily told; maybe thou knowest Tmolus by hearsay.

PENTHEUS I know it, the range that rings the city of Sardis round.

DIONYSUS Thence I come, Lydia is my native home.

PENTHEUS What makes thee bring these mysteries to Hellas?

DIONYSUS Dionysus, the son of Zeus, initiated me.

PENTHEUS Is there a Zeus in Lydia, who begets new gods?

DIONYSUS No, but Zeus who married Semele in Hellas.

PENTHEUS Was it by night or in the face of day that he constrained thee?

DIONYSUS 'Twas face to face he intrusted his mysteries to me.

PENTHEUS Pray, what special feature stamps thy rites?

DIONYSUS That is a secret to be hidden from the uninitiated.

PENTHEUS What profit bring they to their votaries?

DIONYSUS Thou must not be told, though 'tis well worth knowing.

PENTHEUS A pretty piece of trickery, to excite my curiosity!

DIONYSUS A man of godless life is an abomination to the rites of the god.

PENTHEUS Thou sayest thou didst see the god clearly; what was he like?

DIONYSUS What his fancy chose; I was not there to order this.

PENTHEUS Another clever twist and turn of thine, without a word of answer.

DIONYSUS He were a fool, methinks, who would utter wisdom to a fool.

PENTHEUS Hast thou come hither first with this deity?

DIONYSUS All foreigners already celebrate these mysteries with dances.

PENTHEUS The reason being, they are far behind Hellenes in wisdom.

DIONYSUS In this at least far in advance, though their customs differ.

PENTHEUS Is it by night or day thou performest these devotions?

DIONYSUS By night mostly; darkness lends solemnity.

PENTHEUS Calculated to entrap and corrupt women.

DIONYSUS Day too for that matter may discover shame.

PENTHEUS This vile quibbling settles thy punishment.

DIONYSUS Brutish ignorance and godlessness will settle thine.

PENTHEUS How bold our Bacchanal is growing! a very master in this wordy strife!

DIONYSUS Tell me what I am to suffer; what is the grievous doom thou wilt inflict upon me?

PENTHEUS First will I shear off thy dainty tresses.

DIONYSUS My locks are sacred; for the god I let them grow.

PENTHEUS Next surrender that thyrsus.

DIONYSUS Take it from me thyself; 'tis the wand of Dionysus I am bearing.

PENTHEUS In dungeon deep thy body will I guard.

DIONYSUS The god himself will set me free, whene'er I list.

PENTHEUS Perhaps he may, when thou standest amid thy Bacchanals and callest on his name.

DIONYSUS Even now he is near me and witnesses my treatment.

PENTHEUS Why, where is he? To my eyes he is invisible.

DIONYSUS He is by my side; thou art a godless man and therefore dost not see him.

PENTHEUS Seize him! the fellow scorns me and Thebes too.

DIONYSUS I bid you bind me not, reason addressing madness.

PENTHEUS But I say "bind!" with better right than thou.

DIONYSUS Thou hast no knowledge of the life thou art leading; thy very existence is now a mystery to thee.

PENTHEUS I am Pentheus, son of Agave and Echion.

DIONYSUS Well-named to be misfortune's mate!

PENTHEUS Avaunt! Ho! shut him up within the horses' stalls hard by, that for light he may have pitchy gloom. Do thy dancing there, and these women whom thou bringest with thee to share thy villainies I will either sell as slaves or make their hands cease from this noisy beating of drums, and set them to work at the loom as servants of my own.

DIONYSUS I will go; for that which fate forbids, can never befall me. For this thy mockery be sure Dionysus will exact a recompense of thee-even the god whose existence thou deniest; for thou art injuring him by haling me to prison. (Exit DIONYSUS, guarded, and PENTHEUS.)

CHORUS Hail to thee, Dirce, happy maid, daughter revered of Achelous! within thy founts thou didst receive in days gone by the babe of Zeus, what time his father caught him up into his thigh from out the deathless flame, while thus he cried: "Go rest, my Dithyrambus, there within thy father's womb; by this name, O Bacchic god, I now proclaim thee to Thebes." But thou, blest Dirce, thrustest me aside, when in thy midst I strive to hold my revels graced with crowns. Why dost thou scorn me? Why avoid me? By the clustered charm that Dionysus sheds o'er the vintage I vow there yet shall come a time when thou wilt turn thy thoughts to Bromius. What furious rage the earth-born race displays, even Pentheus sprung of a dragon of old, himself the son of earth-born Echion, a savage monster in his very mien, not made in human mould, but like some murderous giant pitted against heaven; for he means to bind me, the handmaid of Bromius, in cords forthwith, and e'en now he keeps my fellow-reveller pent within his palace, plunged in a gloomy dungeon. Dost thou mark this, O Dionysus, son of Zeus, thy prophets struggling 'gainst resistless might? Come, O king, brandishing thy golden thyrsus along the slopes of Olympus; restrain the pride of this bloodthirsty wretch! Oh! where in Nysa, haunt of beasts, or on the peaks of Corycus art thou, Dionysus, marshalling with thy wand the revellers? or haply in the thick forest depths of Olympus, where erst Orpheus with his lute gathered trees to his minstrelsy, and beasts that range the fields. Ah blest Pieria! Evius honours thee, to thee will he come with his Bacchic rites to lead the dance, and thither will he lead the circling Maenads, crossing the swift current of Axius and the Lydias, that giveth wealth and happiness to man, yea, and the father of rivers, which, as I have heard, enriches with his waters fair a land of steeds.

DIONYSUS (Within) What ho! my Bacchantes, ho! hear my call, oh! hear.

CHORUS Who art thou? what Evian cry is this that calls me? whence comes it?

DIONYSUS What ho! once more I call, I the son of Semele, the child of Zeus.

CHORUS II My master, O my master, hail!

CHORUS III Come to our revel-band, O Bromian god.

CHORUS IV Thou solid earth!

CHORUS Most awful shock!

CHORUS VI O horror! soon will the palace of Pentheus totter and fall.

CHORUS VII Dionysus is within this house.

CHORUS VIII Do homage to him.

CHORUS IX We do! I do!

CHORUS Did ye mark yon architrave of stone upon the columns start asunder?

CHORUS XI Within these walls the triumph-shout of Bromius himself will rise.

DIONYSUS Kindle the blazing torch with lightning's fire, abandon to the flames the halls of Pentheus.

CHORUS XII Ha! dost not see the flame, dost not clearly mark it at the sacred tomb of Semele, the lightning flame which long ago the hurler of the bolt left there?

CHORUS XIII Your trembling limbs prostrate, ye Maenads, low upon the ground.

CHORUS XIV Yea, for our king, the son of Zeus, is assailing and utterly confounding this house. (Enter DIONY-SUS.)

DIONYSUS Are ye so stricken with terror that ye have fallen to the earth, O foreign dames? Ye saw then, it would seem, how the Bacchic god made Pentheus' halls to quake; but arise, be of good heart, compose your trembling limbs.

CHORUS O chiefest splendour of our gladsome Bacchic sport, with what joy I see thee in my loneliness!

DIONYSUS Were ye cast down when I was led into the house, to be plunged into the gloomy dungeons of Pentheus?

CHORUS Indeed I was. Who was to protect me, if thou shouldst meet with mishap? But how wert thou set free from the clutches of this godless wretch?

DIONYSUS My own hands worked out my own salvation, easily and without trouble.

CHORUS But did he not lash fast thy hands with cords?

DIONYSUS There too I mocked him; he thinks he bound me, whereas he never touched or caught hold of me, but fed himself on fancy. For at the stall, to which he brought me for a gaol, he found a bull, whose legs and hoofs he straightly tied, breathing out fury the while, the sweat trickling from his body, and he biting his lips; but I from near at hand sat calmly looking on. Meantime came the Bacchic god and made the house quake, and at his mother's tomb relit the fire; but Pentheus, seeing this, thought his palace was ablaze, and hither and thither he rushed, bidding his servants bring water; but all in vain was every servant's busy toil. Thereon he let this labour be awhile, and, thinking maybe that I had escaped, rushed into the palace with his murderous sword unsheathed. Then did Bromius-so at least it seemed to me; I only tell you what I thought-made a phantom in the hall, and he rushed after it in headlong haste, and stabbed the lustrous air, thinking he wounded me. Further the Bacchic god did other outrage to him; he dashed the building to the ground, and there it lies a mass of ruin, a sight to make him rue most bitterly my bonds. At last from sheer fatigue he dropped his sword and fell fainting; for he a mortal frail, dared to wage war upon a god; but I meantime quietly left the house and am come to you, with never a thought of Pentheus. But methinks he will soon appear before the house; at least there is a sound of steps within. What will he say, I wonder, after this? Well, be his fury never so great, I will lightly bear it; for 'tis a wise man's way to school his temper into due control. (Enter PENTHEUS.)

PENTHEUS Shamefully have I been treated; that stranger, whom but now I made so fast in prison, hath escaped me. Ha! there is the man! What means this? How didst thou come forth, to appear thus in front of my palace?

DIONYSUS Stay where thou art; and moderate thy fury.

PENTHEUS How is it thou hast escaped thy fetters and art at large?

DIONYSUS Did I not say, or didst thou not hear me, "There is one will loose me."

PENTHEUS Who was it? there is always something strange in what thou sayest.

DIONYSUS He who makes the clustering vine to grow for man.

PENTHEUS (I scorn him and his vines!)

DIONYSUS A fine taunt indeed thou hurlest here at Dionysus!

PENTHEUS (To his servants) Bar every tower that hems us in, I order you.

DIONYSUS What use? Cannot gods pass even over walls?

PENTHEUS How wise thou art, except where thy wisdom is needed!

DIONYSUS Where most 'tis needed, there am I most wise. But first listen to yonder messenger and hear what he says; he comes from the hills with tidings for thee; and I will await thy pleasure, nor seek to fly. (Enter MESSENGER.) Messenger. Pentheus, ruler of this realm of Thebes! I am come from Cithaeron, where the dazzling flakes of pure white snow ne'er cease to fall.

PENTHEUS What urgent news dost bring me?

MESSENGER I have seen, O king, those frantic Bacchanals, who darted in frenzy from this land with bare white feet, and I am come to tell thee and the city the wondrous deeds they do, deeds passing strange. But I fain would hear, whether I am freely to tell all I saw there, or shorten my story; for I fear thy hasty temper, sire, thy sudden bursts of wrath and more than princely rage.

PENTHEUS Say on, for thou shalt go unpunished by me in all respects; for to be angered with the upright is wrong. The direr thy tale about the Bacchantes, the heavier punishment will I inflict on this fellow who brought his secret arts amongst our women.

MESSENGER I was just driving the herds of kine to a ridge of the hill as I fed them, as the sun shot forth his rays and made the earth grow warm; when lo! I see three revel-bands of women; Autonoe was chief of one, thy mother Agave of the second, while Ino's was the third. There they lay asleep, all tired out; some were resting on branches of the pine, others had laid their heads in careless ease on oak-leaves piled upon the ground, observing all modesty; not, as thou sayest, seeking to gratify their lusts alone amid the woods, by wine and soft flute-music maddened.

Anon in their midst thy mother uprose and cried aloud to wake them from their sleep, when she heard the lowing of my horned kine. And up they started to their feet, brushing from their eyes sleep's quickening dew, a wondrous sight of grace and modesty, young and old and maidens yet unwed. First o'er their shoulders they let stream their hair; then all did gird their fawn-skins up, who hitherto had left the fastenings loose, girdling the dappled hides with snakes that licked their cheeks. Others fondled in their arms gazelles or savage whelps of wolves, and suckled them-young mothers these with babes at home, whose breasts were still full of milk; crowns they wore of ivy or of oak or blossoming convolvulus. And one took her thyrsus and struck it into the earth, and forth there gushed a limpid spring; and another plunged her wand into the lap of earth and there the god sent up a fount of wine; and all who wished for draughts of milk had but to scratch the soil with their finger-tips and there they had it in abundance, while from every ivy-wreathed staff sweet rills of honey trickled.

Hadst thou been there and seen this, thou wouldst have turned to pray to the god, whom now thou dost disparage. Anon we herdsmen and shepherds met to discuss their strange and wondrous doings; then one, who wandereth oft to town and hath a trick of speech, made harangue in the midst, "O ye who dwell upon the hallowed mountain-terraces! shall we chase Agave, mother of Pentheus, from her Bacchic rites, and thereby do our prince a service?" We liked his speech, and placed ourselves in hidden ambush among the leafy thickets; they at the appointed time began to wave the thyrsus for their Bacchic rites, calling on Iacchus, the Bromian god, the son of Zeus, in united chorus, and the whole mount and the wild creatures re-echoed their cry; all nature stirred as they rushed on. Now Agave chanced to come springing near me, so up I leapt from out my ambush where I lay concealed, meaning to seize her. But she cried out, "What ho! my nimble hounds, here are men upon our track; but follow me, ay, follow, with the thyrsus in your hand for weapon." Thereat we fled, to escape being torn in pieces by the Bacchantes; but they, with hands that bore no weapon of steel, attacked our cattle as they browsed. Then wouldst thou have seen Agave mastering some sleek lowing calf, while others rent the heifers limb from limb. Before thy eyes there would have been hurling of ribs and hoofs this way and that; and strips of flesh, all blood-bedabbled, dripped as they hung from the pine-branches. Wild bulls, that glared but now with rage along their horns, found themselves tripped up, dragged down to earth by countless maidens' hands. The flesh upon their limbs was stripped therefrom quicker than thou couldst have closed thy royal eye-lids. Then off they sped, like birds that skim the air, to the plains beneath the hills, which bear a fruitful harvest for Thebes beside the waters of Asopus; to Hysiae and Erythrae, hamlets 'neath Cithaeron's peak, with fell intent, swooping on everything and scattering all pellmell; and they would snatch children from their homes; but all that they placed upon their shoulders, abode there firmly without being tied, and fell not to the dusky earth, not even brass or iron; and on their hair they carried fire and it burnt them not; but the country-folk rushed to arms, furious at being pillaged by Bacchanals; whereon ensued, O king, this wondrous spectacle. For though the ironshod dart would draw no blood from them, they with the thyrsus, which they hurled, caused many a wound and put their foes to utter rout, women chasing men, by some god's intervention. Then they returned to the place whence they had started, even to the springs the god had made to spout for them; and there washed off the blood, while serpents with their tongues were licking clean each gout from their cheeks. Wherefore, my lord and master, receive this deity, whoe'er he be, within the city; for, great as he is in all else, I have likewise heard men say, 'twas he that gave the vine to man, sorrow's antidote. Take wine away and Cypris flies, and every other human joy is dead.

CHORUS Though I fear to speak my mind with freedom in the presence of my king, still must I utter this; Dionysus yields to no deity in might.

PENTHEUS Already, look you! the presumption of these Bacchantes is upon us, swift as fire, a sad disgrace in the eyes of all Hellas. No time for hesitation now! away to the Electra gate! order a muster of all my men-at-arms, of those that mount fleet steeds, of all who brandish light bucklers, of archers too that make the bowstring twang; for I will march against the Bacchanals. By Heaven I this passes all, if we are to be thus treated by women. (Exit MESSENGER.)

DIONYSUS Still obdurate, O Pentheus, after hearing my words! In spite of all the evil treatment I am enduring from thee, still I warn thee of the sin of bearing arms against a god, and bid thee cease; for Bromius will not endure thy driving his votaries from the mountains where they revel.

PENTHEUS A truce to thy preaching to me! thou hast escaped thy bonds, preserve thy liberty; else will I renew thy punishment.

DIONYSUS I would rather do him sacrifice than in a fury kick against the pricks; thou a mortal, he a god.

PENTHEUS Sacrifice! that will I, by setting afoot a wholesale slaughter of women 'mid Cithaeron's glens, as they deserve.

DIONYSUS Ye will all be put to flight-a shameful thing that they with the Bacchic thyrsus should rout your mail-clad warriors.

PENTHEUS I find this stranger a troublesome foe to encounter; doing or suffering he is alike irrepressible.

DIONYSUS Friend, there is still a way to compose this bitterness.

PENTHEUS Say how; am I to serve my own servants?

DIONYSUS I will bring the women hither without weapons.

PENTHEUS Ha! ha! this is some crafty scheme of thine against me.

DIONYSUS What kind of scheme, if by my craft I purpose to save thee?

PENTHEUS You have combined with them to form this plot, that your revels may on for ever.

DIONYSUS Nay, but this is the compact I made with the god; be sure of that.

PENTHEUS (Preparing to start forth) Bring forth my

arms. Not another word from thee!

DIONYSUS Ha! wouldst thou see them seated on the hills?

PENTHEUS Of all things, yes! I would give untold sums for that.

DIONYSUS Why this sudden, strong desire?

PENTHEUS 'Twill be a bitter sight, if I find them drunk with wine.

DIONYSUS And would that be a pleasant sight which will prove bitter to thee?

PENTHEUS Believe me, yes! beneath the fir-trees as I sit in silence.

DIONYSUS Nay, they will track thee, though thou come secretly.

PENTHEUS Well, I will go openly; thou wert right to say so.

DIONYSUS Am I to be thy guide? wilt thou essay the road?

PENTHEUS Lead on with all speed, I grudge thee all delay.

DIONYSUS Array thee then in robes of fine linen.

PENTHEUS Why so? Am I to enlist among women after being a man?

DIONYSUS They may kill thee, if thou show thy manhood there.

PENTHEUS Well said! Thou hast given me a taste of thy wit already.

DIONYSUS Dionysus schooled me in this lore.

PENTHEUS How am I to carry out thy wholesome advice?

DIONYSUS Myself will enter thy palace and robe thee.

PENTHEUS What is the robe to be? a woman's? Nay, I am ashamed.

DIONYSUS Thy eagerness to see the Maenads goes no further.

PENTHEUS But what dress dost say thou wilt robe me in?

DIONYSUS Upon thy head will I make thy hair grow long.

PENTHEUS Describe my costume further.

DIONYSUS Thou wilt wear a robe reaching to thy feet; and on thy head shall be a snood.

PENTHEUS Wilt add aught else to my attire?

DIONYSUS A thyrsus in thy hand, and a dappled fawn-skin.

PENTHEUS I can never put on woman's dress.

DIONYSUS Then wilt thou cause bloodshed by coming to blows with the Bacchanals.

PENTHEUS Thou art right. Best go spy upon them first.

DIONYSUS Well, e'en that is wiser than by evil means to follow evil ends.

PENTHEUS But how shall I pass through the city of the Cadmeans unseen?

DIONYSUS We will go by unfrequented paths. I will lead the way.

PENTHEUS Anything rather than that the Bacchantes should laugh at me.

DIONYSUS We will enter the palace and consider the proper steps.

PENTHEUS Thou hast my leave. I am all readiness. I will enter, prepared to set out either sword in hand or following thy advice. (Exit PENTHEUS.)

DIONYSUS Women! our prize is nearly in the net. Soon shall he reach the Bacchanals, and there pay forfeit with his life. O Dionysus! now 'tis thine to act, for thou art not far away; let us take vengeance on him. First drive him mad by fixing in his soul a wayward frenzy; for never, whilst his senses are his own, will he consent to don a woman's dress; but when his mind is gone astray he will put it on. And fain would I make him a laughing-stock to Thebes as he is led in woman's dress through the city, after those threats with which he menaced me before. But I will go to array Pentheus in those robes which he shall wear when he sets out for Hades' halls, a victim to his own mother's fury; so shall he recognize Dionysus, the son of Zeus, who proves himself at last a god most terrible, for all his gentleness to man. (Exit DIONYSUS.)

CHORUS Will this white foot e'er join the night-long dance? what time in Bacchic ecstasy I toss my neck to heaven's dewy breath, like a fawn, that gambols 'mid the meadow's green delights, when she hath escaped the fearful chase, clear of the watchers, o'er the woven nets; while the huntsman, with loud halloo, harks on his hounds' full cry, and she with laboured breath at lightning speed bounds o'er the level water-meadows, glad to be far from man amid the foliage of the bosky grove. What is true wisdom, or what fairer boon has heaven placed in mortals' reach, than to gain the mastery o'er a fallen foe? What is fair is dear for aye. Though slow be its advance, yet surely moves the power of the gods, correcting those mortal wights, that court a senseless pride, or, in the madness of their fancy, disregard the gods. Subtly they lie in wait, through the long march of time, and so hunt down the godless man. For it is never right in theory or in practice to o'erride the law of custom. This is a maxim cheaply bought: whatever comes of God, or in time's long annals, has grown into a law upon a natural basis, this is sovereign. What is true wisdom, or what fairer boon has heaven placed in mortals' reach, than to gain the mastery o'er a fallen foe? What is fair is dear for aye. Happy is he who hath escaped the wave from out the sea, and reached the haven; and happy he who hath triumphed o'er his troubles; though one surpasses another in wealth and power; yet there be myriad hopes for all the myriad minds; some end in happiness for man, and others come to naught; but him, whose life from day to day is blest, I deem a happy man. (Enter DIONYSUS.)

DIONYSUS Ho! Pentheus, thou that art so eager to see what is forbidden, and to show thy zeal in an unworthy cause, come forth before the palace, let me see thee clad as a woman in frenzied Bacchante's dress, to spy upon thy own mother and her company. (Enter PENTHEUS.) Yes, thou resemblest closely a daughter of Cadmus.

PENTHEUS Of a truth I seem to see two suns, and two towns of Thebes, our seven-gated city; and thou, methinks, art a bull going before to guide me, and on thy head a pair of horns have grown. Wert thou really once a brute beast? Thon hast at any rate the appearance of a bull.

DIONYSUS The god attends us, ungracious heretofore, but now our sworn friend; and now thine eyes behold the things they should.

PENTHEUS Pray, what do I resemble? Is not mine the carriage of Ino, or Agave my own mother?

DIONYSUS In seeing thee, I seem to see them in person. But this tress is straying from its place, no longer as I bound it 'neath the snood.

PENTHEUS I disarranged it from its place as I tossed it to and fro within my chamber, in Bacchic ecstasy.

DIONYSUS Well, I will rearrange it, since to tend thee is my care; hold up thy head.

PENTHEUS Come, put it straight; for on thee do I depend.

DIONYSUS Thy girdle is loose, and the folds of thy dress

do not hang evenly below thy ankles.

PENTHEUS I agree to that as regards the right side, but on the other my dress hangs straight with my foot.

DIONYSUS Surely thou wilt rank me first among thy friends, when contrary to thy expectation thou findest the Bacchantes virtuous.

PENTHEUS Shall I hold the thyrsus in the right or left hand to look most like a Bacchanal?

DIONYSUS Hold it in thy right hand, and step out with thy right foot; thy change of mind compels thy praise.

PENTHEUS Shall I be able to carry on my shoulders Cithaeron's glens, the Bacchanals and all?

DIONYSUS Yes, if so thou wilt; for though thy mind was erst diseased, 'tis now just as it should be.

PENTHEUS Shall we take levers, or with my hands can I uproot it, thrusting arm or shoulder 'neath its peaks?

DIONYSUS No, no! destroy not the seats of the Nymphs and the haunts of Pan, the place of his piping.

PENTHEUS Well said! Women must not be mastered by brute force; amid the pines will I conceal myself.

DIONYSUS Thou shalt hide thee in the place that fate appoints, coming by stealth to spy upon the Bacchanals.

PENTHEUS Why, methinks they are already caught in the pleasant snares of dalliance, like birds amid the brakes.

DIONYSUS Set out with watchful heed then for this very purpose; maybe thou wilt catch them, if thou be not first caught thyself.

PENTHEUS Conduct me through the very heart of Thebes, for I am the only man among them bold enough to do this deed.

DIONYSUS Thou alone bearest thy country's burden,

thou and none other; wherefore there await thee such struggles as needs must. Follow me, for I will guide thee safely thither; another shall bring thee thence.

PENTHEUS My mother maybe.

DIONYSUS For every eye to see.

PENTHEUS My very purpose in going.

DIONYSUS Thou shalt be carried back,

PENTHEUS What luxury

DIONYSUS In thy mother's arms.

PENTHEUS Thou wilt e'en force me into luxury.

DIONYSUS Yes, to luxury such as this.

PENTHEUS Truly, the task I am undertaking deserves it. (Exit PENTHEUS.)

DIONYSUS Strange, ah! strange is thy career, leading to scenes of woe so strange, that thou shalt achieve a fame that towers to heaven. Stretch forth thy hands, Agave, and ye her sisters, daughters of Cadmus; mighty is the strife to which I am bringing the youthful king, and the victory shall rest with me and Bromius; all else the event will show. (Exit DIONYSUS.)

CHORUS To the hills! to the hills! fleet hounds of madness, where the daughters of Cadmus hold their revels, goad them into wild fury against the man disguised in woman's dress, a frenzied spy upon the Maenads. First shall his mother mark him as he peers from some smooth rock or riven tree, and thus to the Maenads she will call, "Who is this of Cadmus' sons comes hasting to the mount, to the mountain away, to spy on us, my Bacchanals? Whose child can he be? For he was never born of woman's blood; but from some lioness maybe or Libyan Gorgon is he sprung." Let justice appear and show herself, sword in hand, to plunge it through and through the throat of the godless, lawless, impious son of Echion, earth's monstrous child! who with wicked heart and lawless rage, with mad intent and frantic purpose, sets out to meddle with thy holy rites, and with thy mother's, Bacchic god, thinking with his weak arm to master might as masterless as thine. This is the life that saves all pain, if a man confine his thoughts to human themes, as is his mortal nature, making no pretence where heaven is concerned. I envy not deep subtleties; far other joys have I, in tracking out great truths writ clear from all eternity, that a man should live his life by day and night in purity and holiness, striving toward a noble goal, and should honour the gods by casting from him each ordinance that lies outside the pale of right. Let justice show herself, advancing sword in hand to plunge it through and through the throat of Echion's son, that godless, lawless, and abandoned child of earth! Appear, O Bacchus, to our eyes as a bull or serpent with a hundred heads, or take the shape of a lion breathing flame! Oh! come, and with a mocking smile cast the deadly noose about the hunter of thy Bacchanals, e'en as he swoops upon the Maenads gathered yonder. (Enter SECOND MESSENGER.)

SECOND MESSENGER O house, so prosperous once through Hellas long ago, home of the old Sidonian prince, who sowed the serpent's crop of earth-born men, how do I mourn thee! slave though I be, yet still the sorrows of his master touch a good slave's heart.

CHORUS How now? Hast thou fresh tidings of the Bacchantes?

SECOND MESSENGER Pentheus, Echion's son is dead.

CHORUS Bromius, my king! now art thou appearing in thy might divine.

SECOND MESSENGER Ha! what is it thou sayest? art thou glad, woman, at my master's misfortunes?

CHORUS A stranger I, and in foreign tongue I express my joy, for now no more do I cower in terror of the chain.

SECOND MESSENGER Dost think Thebes so poor in men?(*, * Probably the whole of one iambic line with part of another is here lost.)

CHORUS 'Tis Dionysus, Dionysus, not Thebes that lords it over me.

SECOND MESSENGER All can I pardon thee save this; to exult o'er hopeless suffering is sorry conduct, dames.

CHORUS Tell me, oh! tell me how he died, that villain scheming villainy!

SECOND MESSENGER Soon as we had left the home-steads of this Theban land and had crossed the streams of Asopus, we began to breast Cithaeron's heights, Pentheus and I, for I went with my master, and the stranger too, who was to guide us to the scene. First then we sat us down in a grassy glen, carefully silencing each footfall and whispered breath, to see without being seen. Now there was a dell walled in by rocks, with rills to water it, and shady pines o'erhead; there were the Maenads seated, busied with joyous toils. Some were wreathing afresh the drooping thyrsus with curling ivy-sprays; others, like colts let loose from the carved chariot-yoke, were answering each other in hymns of Bacchic rapture. But Pentheus, son of sorrow, seeing not the women gathered there, exclaimed, "Sir stranger, from where I stand, I cannot clearly see the mock Bacchantes; but I will climb a hillock or a soaring pine whence to see clearly the shameful doings of the Bacchanals." Then and there I saw the stranger work a miracle; for catching a lofty fir-branch by the very end he drew it downward to the dusky earth, lower yet and ever lower; and like a bow it bent, or rounded wheel, whose curving circle grows complete, as chalk and line describe it; e'en so the stranger drew down the mountain-branch between his hands, bending it to earth, by more than human agency. And when he had seated Pentheus aloft on the pine branches, he let them slip through his hands gently, careful not to shake him from his seat. Up soared the branch straight into the air above, with my master perched thereon, seen by the Maenads better far than he saw them; for scarce was he beheld upon his lofty throne, when the stranger disappeared, while from the sky there came a voice, 'twould seem, by Dionysus uttered-

"Maidens, I bring the man who tried to mock you and me and my mystic rites; take vengeance on him." And as he spake he raised 'twixt heaven and earth a dazzling column of awful flame. Hushed grew the sky, and still hung each leaf throughout the grassy glen, nor couldst thou have heard one creature cry. But they, not sure of the voice they heard, sprang up and peered all round; then once again his bidding came; and when the daughters of Cadmus knew it was the Bacchic god in very truth that called, swift as doves they dirted off in cager haste, his mother Agave and her sisters dear and all the Bacchanals; through torrent glen, o'er boulders huge they bounded on, inspired with madness by the god. Soon as they saw my master perched upon the fir, they set to hurling stones at him with all their might, mounting a commanding eminence, and with pine-branches he was pelted as with darts; and others shot their wands through the air at Pentheus, their hapless target, but all to no purpose. For there he sat beyond the reach of their hot endeavours, a helpless, hopeless victim. At last they rent off limbs from oaks and were for prising up the roots with levers not of iron. But when they still could make no end to all their toil, Agave cried: "Come stand around, and grip the sapling trunk, my Bacchanals! that we may catch the beast that sits thereon, lest he divulge the secrets of our god's religion."

Then were a thousand hands laid on the fir, and from the ground they tore it up, while he from his seat aloft came tumbling to the ground with lamentations long and loud, e'en Pentheus; for well he knew his hour was come. His mother first, a priestess for the nonce, began the bloody deed and fell upon him; whereon he tore the snood from off his hair, that hapless Agave might recognize and spare him, crying as he touched her cheek, "O mother! it is I, thy own son Pentheus, the child thou didst bear in Echion's halls; have pity on me, mother dear! oh! do not for any sin of mine slay thy own son."

But she, the while, with foaming mouth and wildly rolling eyes, bereft of reason as she was, heeded him not; for the god possessed her. And she caught his left hand in her grip, and planting her foot upon her victim's trunk she tore the shoulder from its socket, not of her own strength, but the god made it an easy task to her hands; and Ino set to work upon the other side, rending the flesh with Autonoe and all the eager host of Bacchanals; and one united cry arose, the victim's groans while yet he breathed, and their triumphant shouts. One would make an arm her prey, another a foot with the sandal on it; and his ribs were stripped of flesh by their rending nails; and each one with blood-dabbled hands was tossing Pentheus' limbs about. Scattered lies his corpse, part beneath the rugged rocks, and part amid the deep dark woods, no easy task to find; but his poor head hath his mother made her own, and fixing it upon the point of a thyrsus, as it had been a mountain lion's, she bears it through the midst of Cithaeron, having left her sisters with the Maenads at their rites. And she is entering these walls exulting in her hunting fraught with woe, calling on the Bacchic god her fellow-hunter who had helped her to triumph in a chase, where her only prize was tears.

But I will get me hence, away from this piteous scene, before Agave reach the palace. To my mind self-restraint and reverence for the things of God point alike the best and wisest course for all mortals who pursue them. (Exit SECOND MESSENGER.)

CHORUS Come, let us exalt our Bacchic god in choral strain, let us loudly chant the fall of Pentheus from the serpent sprung, who assumed a woman's dress and took the fair Bacchic wand, sure pledge of death, with a bull to guide him to his doom. O ye Bacchanals of Thebes! glorious is the triumph ye have achieved, ending in sorrow and tears. 'Tis a noble enterprise to dabble the hand in the blood of a son till it drips. But hist! I see Agave, the mother of Pentheus, with wild rolling eye hasting to the house; welcome the revellers of the Bacchic god. (Enter AGAVE.)

AGAVE Ye Bacchanals from Asia

CHORUS Why dost thou rouse me? why?

AGAVE From the hills I am bringing to my home a tendril freshly-culled, glad guerdon-of the chase.

CHORUS I see it, and I will welcome thee unto our revels. All hail!

AGAVE I caught him with never a snare, this lion's whelp, as ye may see.

CHORUS From what desert lair?

AGAVE Cithaeron-

CHORUS Yes, Cithaeron?

AGAVE Was his death.

CHORUS Who was it gave the first blow?

AGAVE Mine that privilege; "Happy Agave!" they call me 'mid our revellers.

CHORUS Who did the rest?

AGAVE Cadmus-

CHORUS What of him?

AGAVE His daughters struck the monster after me; yes, after me.

CHORUS Fortune smiled upon thy hunting here.

AGAVE Come, share the banquet.

CHORUS Share? ah I what?

AGAVE 'Tis but a tender whelp, the down just sprouting on its cheek beneath a crest of failing hair.

CHORUS The hair is like some wild creature's.

AGAVE The Bacchic god, a hunter skilled, roused his Maenads to pursue this quarry skilfully.

CHORUS Yea, our king is a hunter indeed.

AGAVE Dost approve?

CHORUS Of course I do.

AGAVE Soon shall the race of Cadmus-

CHORUS And Pentheus, her own son, shall to his mother-

AGAVE Offer praise for this her quarry of the lion's brood.

CHORUS Quarry strange!

AGAVE And strangely caught.

CHORUS Dost thou exult?

AGAVE Right glad am I to have achieved a great and glorious triumph for my land that all can see.

CHORUS Alas for thee! show to the folk the booty thou hast won and art bringing hither.

AGAVE All ye who dwell in fair fenced Thebes, draw near that ye may see the fierce wild beast that we daughters of Cadmus made our prey, not with the thong-thrown darts of Thessaly, nor yet with snares, but with our fingers fair. Ought men idly to boast and get them armourers' weapons? when we with these our hands have caught this prey and torn the monster limb from limb? Where is my aged sire? let him approach. And where is Pentheus, my son? Let him bring a ladder and raise it against the house to nail up on the gables this lion's head, my booty from the chase. (Enter CADMUS.)

CADMUS Follow me, servants to the palace-front, with your sad burden in your arms, ay, follow, with the corpse of Pentheus, which after long weary search I found, as ye see it, torn to pieces amid Cithaeron's glens, and am bringing hither; no two pieces did I find together, as they lay scattered through the trackless wood. For I heard what awful deeds one of my daughters had done, just as I entered the city-walls with old Teiresias returning from the Bacchanals;

so I turned again unto the and bring from thence my son who was slain by Maenads. There I saw Autonoe, that bare Actaeon on a day to Aristaeus, and Ino with her, still ranging the oak-groves in their unhappy frenzy; but one told me that that Agave, was rushing wildly hither, nor was it idly said, for there I see her, sight of woe!

AGAVE Father, loudly mayst thou boast, that the daughters thou hast begotten are far the best of mortal race; of one and all I speak, though chiefly of myself, who left my shuttle at the loom for nobler enterprise, even to hunt savage beasts with my hands; and in my arms I bring my prize, as thou seest, that it may be nailed up on thy palace-wall; take it, father, in thy had and proud of my hunting, call thy friends to a banquet; for blest art thou, ah! doubly blest in these our gallant exploits.

CADMUS O grief that has no bounds, too cruel for mortal eye! 'tis murder ye have done with your hapless hands. Fair is the victim thou hast offered to the gods, inviting me and my Thebans to the feast Ah, woe is me first for thy sorrows, then for mine. What ruin the god, the Bromian king, hath brought on us, just maybe, but too severe, seeing he is our kinsman!

AGAVE How peevish old age makes men! what sullen looks! Oh, may my son follow in his mother's footsteps and be as lucky in his hunting, when he goes quest of game in company with Theban youthsl But he can do naught but wage war with gods. Father, 'tis thy duty to warn him. Who will summon him hither to my sight to witness my happiness?

CADMUS Alas for you! alas! Terrible will be your grief when ye are conscious of your deeds; could ye re. for ever till life's close in your present state, ye would not, spite of ruined bliss, appear so cursed with woe.

AGAVE Why? what is faulty bere? what here for sorrow?

CADMUS First let thine eye look up to heaven.

AGAVE See! I do so. Why dost thou suggest my looking thereupon?

CADMUS Is it still the same, or dost think there's any change?

AGAVE 'Tis brighter than it was, and dearer too.

CADMUS Is there still that wild unrest within thy soul?

AGAVE I know not what thou sayest now; yet methinks my brain is clearing, and my former frenzy passed away.

CADMUS Canst understand, and give distinct replies?

AGAVE Father, how completely I forget all we said before!

CADMUS To what house wert thou brought with marriage-hymns?

AGAVE Thou didst give me to earthborn Echion, as men call him.

CADMUS What child was born thy husband in his halls?

AGAVE Pentheus, of my union with his father.

CADMUS What head is that thou barest in thy arms?

AGAVE A lion's; at least they said so, who hunted it.

CADMUS Consider it aright; 'tis no great task to look at it.

AGAVE Ah! what do I see? what is this I am carrying in my hands?

CADMUS Look closely at it; make thy knowledge more certain.

AGAVE Ah, 'woe is me! O sight of awful sorrow!

CADMUS Dost think it like a lion's head?

AGAVE Ah no! 'tis Pentheus' head which I his unhappy

mother hold.

CADMUS Bemoaned by me, or ever thou didst recognize him.

AGAVE Who slew him? How came he into my hands?

CADMUS O piteous truth! how ill-timed thy presence here!

AGAVE Speak; my bosom throbs at this suspense.

CADMUS 'Twas thou didst slay him, thou and thy sisters.

AGAVE Where died he? in the house or where?

CADMUS On the very spot where hounds of yore rent Actaeon in pieces.

AGAVE Why went he, wretched youth! to Cithaeron?

CADMUS He would go and mock the god and thy Bacchic rites.

AGAVE But how was it we had journeyed thither?

CADMUS Ye were distraught; the whole city had the Bacchic frenzy.

AGAVE 'Twas Dionysus proved our ruin; now I see it all.

CADMUS Yes, for the slight he suffered; ye would not believe in his godhead.

AGAVE Father, where is my dear child's corpse?

CADMUS With toil I searched it out and am bringing it myself.

AGAVE Is it all fitted limb to limb in seemly wise? CADMUS (*, * One line, or maybe more, is missing)

AGAVE But what had Pentheus to do with folly of mine?

CADMUS He was like you in refusing homage to the god, who, therefore, hath involved you all in one common ruin, you and him alike, to destroy this house and me, forasmuch as I, that had no sons, behold this youth, the fruit of thy womb, unhappy mother! foully and most shamefully slain. To thee, my child, our house looked up, to thee my daughter's son, the stay of my palace, inspiring the city with awe; none caring to flout the old king when he saw thee by, for he would get his deserts. But now shall I be cast out dishonoured from my halls, Cadmus the great, who sowed the crop of Theban seed and reaped that goodly harvest. O beloved child! dead though thou art, thou still shalt be counted by me amongst my own dear children; no more wilt thou lay thy hand upon my chin in fond embrace, my child, and calling on thy mother's sire demand, "Who wrongs thee or dishonours thee, old sire? who vexes thy heart, a thorn within thy side? Speak, that I may punish thy oppressor, father mine!"

But now am I in sorrow plunged, and woe is thee, and woe thy mother and her suffering sisters too! Ah! if there be any man that scorns the gods, let him well mark this prince's death and then believe in them.

CHORUS Cadmus, I am sorry for thy fate; for though thy daughter's child hath met but his deserts, 'tis bitter grief to thee.

AGAVE O father, thou seest how sadly my fortune is changed.(*, * After this a very large lacuna occurs in the MS.)

DIONYSUS Thou shalt be changed into a serpent; and thy wife Harmonia, Ares' child, whom thou in thy human life didst wed, shall change her nature for a snake's, and take its form. With her shalt thou, as leader of barbarian tribes, drive thy team of steers, so saith an oracle of Zeus; and many a city shalt thou sack with an army numberless; but in the day they plunder the oracle of Loxias, shall they rue their homeward march; but thee and Harmonia will Ares rescue, and set thee to live henceforth in the land of the blessed. This do I declare, I Dionysus, son of no mortal father but of Zeus.

Had ye learnt wisdom when ye would not, ye would now be happy with the son of Zeus for your ally.

AGAVE O Dionysus! we have sinned; thy pardon we implore.

DIONYSUS Too late have ye learnt to know me; ye knew me not at the proper time.

AGAVE We recognize our error; but thou art too revengeful.

DIONYSUS Yea, for I, though a god, was slighted by you.

AGAVE Gods should not let their passion sink to man's level.

DIONYSUS Long ago my father Zeus ordained it thus.

AGAVE Alas! my aged sire, our doom is fixed; 'tis woful exile.

DIONYSUS Why then delay the inevitable? Exit.

CADMUS Daughter, to what an awful pass are we now come, thou too, poor child, and thy sisters, while I alas! in my old age must seek barbarian shores, to sojourn there; but the oracle declares that I shall yet lead an army, half-barbarian, half-Hellene, to Hellas; and in serpent's shape shall I carry my wife Harmonia, the daughter of Ares, transformed like me to a savage snake, against the altars and tombs of Hellas at the head of my troops; nor shall I ever cease from my woes, ah me! nor ever cross the downward stream of Acheron and be at rest.

AGAVE Father, I shall be parted from thee and exiled.

CADMUS Alas! my child, why fling thy arms around me, as a snowy cygnet folds its wings about the frail old swan?

AGAVE Whither can I turn, an exile from my country?

CADMUS I know not, my daughter; small help is thy father now.

AGAVE Farewell, my home! farewell, my native city! with sorrow I am leaving thee, an exile from my bridal bower.

CADMUS Go, daughter, to the house of Aristaeus,(*, * Another large lacuna follows.)

AGAVE Father, I mourn for thee.

CADMUS And I for thee, my child; for thy sisters too I shed a tear.

AGAVE Ah! terribly was king Dionysus bringing this outrage on thy house.

CADMUS Yea, for he suffered insults dire from you, his name receiving no meed of honour in Thebes.

AGAVE Farewell, father mine!

CADMUS Farewell, my hapless daughter and yet thou scarce canst reach that bourn.

AGAVE Oh! lead me, guide me to the place where I shall find my sisters, sharers in my exile to their sorrow! Oh! to reach a spot where cursed Cithaeron ne'er shall see me more nor I Cithaeron with mine eyes; where no memorial of the thyrsus is set up! Be they to other Bacchantes dear!

CHORUS Many are the forms the heavenly will assumes, and many a thing the gods fulfil contrary to all hope; that which was expected is not brought to pass, while for the unlooked-for Heaven finds out a way. E'en such hath been the issue here. (Exeunt OMNES.)

THE END

Made in the USA
Lexington, KY
20 July 2019